TEXIT

WHY AND HOW **TEXAS** WILL LEAVE THE UNION

DANIEL MILLER

OTHER WORKS BY DANIEL MILLER

Line in the Sand: The Case for Texas Nationalism

Original publication 2011
Second Edition – May 2018

In *Line in the Sand*, Daniel Miller tackles the concepts of "political will" and "nationalism" and what they mean to Texans. He eloquently removes all reasons for doubt concerning Texas independence and explains that maintaining the status quo is unwise and it is not the way of a statesman, particularly a Texas statesman. Miller shows why, in today's modern age, any method to seek independence other than the ballot box is doomed. *Line in the Sand* is the magnum opus of the Texas independence movement, laying out its mission, goals, and plans to achieve independence peacefully.

Note: *Line in the Sand* has been revised and re-edited. It will be re-released by Defiance Press and Publishing soon after the release of *Texit*.

TEXIT

WHY AND HOW TEXAS WILL LEAVE THE UNION

DANIEL MILLER

DEFIANCE PRESS
& PUBLISHING

ISBN-13: 978-1-948035-08-8 (Hard Cover)
ISBN-13: 978-1-948035-69-9 (Paper Back)
ISBN-13: 978-1-948035-09-5 (eBook)

Library of Congress Control Number: 2018932283

Published in the Republic of Texas by Defiance Press & Publishing, LLC

Printed in Canada

Editing by Janet Musick
Interior designed by Deborah Stocco

Distributed by Midpoint Trade Books

Bulk orders of this book may be obtained by contacting Defiance Press & Publishing at **www.defiancepress.com** or Midpoint Trade Books at **www.midpointtrade.com**

Daniel Miller is president of the Texas Nationalist Movement (https://texasnationalist.com).

Publicity Contact: mfoster@reliantpr.com

DEDICATION

This work is dedicated to my wife, Cara, whose commitment reminds me daily that we are one day closer to Texas independence. It is also dedicated to Charlie Doreck and Lauren Savage, who never gave up on the vision of an independent Republic of Texas.

TABLE OF CONTENTS

> **"**I never despaired of the Republic, but with unshaken confidence in the strength of our cause, and with full knowledge of what the energies of a free and determined people were capable of achieving, I raised my feeble voice!**"**

Mirabeau Lamar, Second President of the Republic of Texas

PREFACE

On August 24, 1996, I set out on a journey that would consume much of my adult life. That was the day I was introduced to the idea that Texas could and should be an independent nation. At that time, tens of thousands of people had signed on to the cause. I was not the first. I wasn't even among the early ones. However, the idea of an independent Republic of Texas struck a chord in me that, to this day, has not been silenced.

In those days, to speak the words "Texas independence" was considered blasphemy of the highest order. Such was the power of that idea that some of the greatest injustices were perpetrated on people like us. Many lost their jobs and their businesses. Many lost their families because they were consumed by their passion for the ideal. Some were persecuted by the government. Others were the object of vilification by the media. We were called criminals and terrorists merely for expressing an idea that was, at the time, extremely unorthodox. Under enormous pressure, and lacking the fortitude of our ancestors, many fell away.

Some, like me, persisted. As we persisted, the idea continued to smolder in the hearts and minds of a population groaning under the weight of an ever-expanding federal government that grew increasingly out of control. Soon, faux solutions pitched as reform evaporated along with the hopes of Texans for a solution within the Union, and the smoldering ignited into a burning desire for something better, something greater.

With time, patience, discipline, and work, more Texans began to see an independent Texas as a viable path forward to preserve the freedoms they cherished and to reach for a future worthy of coming generations that will have to live it as their present. Today, many see independence as the only way to protect the fundamental principles we once called America.

It is not up to me, through this book, to vindicate those who have worked for Texas independence. Future generations will be the judge. Instead, my job is to explain Texit as I know it—hopeful, strong, rooted in Texas history and culture, with its eyes set on the future.

While the amount of information on Texit and the case for it is greater than ever, the discussion has not been elevated accordingly. The pro-independence side has been reduced to shouting "SECEDE!" at every new federal grievance. The opposition has been reduced to the one-sentence reply of, "You can't do that."

Until this point, no single work has addressed the underlying causes driving Texans to support Texit in record numbers, the global political trends shaping the Texit discussion, the imminent implosion of the federal system that will leave the United States powerless to stop Texit, the process under which Texit can occur, or what a newly independent Republic of Texas may look like.

While this book is meant to touch on these issues, it is not comprehensive. Twenty years of exhaustive research on the issue, coupled with the practical experience that comes with working to make Texit a reality, has shown that the entire issue is far too complex for one book. It is, however, a good way to get the conversation started. While this book cannot answer every question about Texit, it does answer some of the most frequent. More important, it provides appropriate context to help the reader understand that the solutions are not unique nor are the challenges insurmountable. It truly is about looking at Texit from a larger perspective and coming to grips with the fact that any perceived barrier to achieving Texas independence has already been broken by someone at some time.

I fully intend for this book to generate controversy. It is in the best interest of Texans and, frankly, all States of the United States if it does. Controversy and criticism create debate and discussion and, in turn, generate more questions. At this point in our history, everyone should be asking more questions, especially about how we are governed.

While this book focuses on Texas, discussions about self-government and self-determination are not, and should not, be limited to Texans. The issues raised should be discussed across every kitchen table and every political campaign across the United States. People everywhere have a fundamental right to ask whether they are being served by their current form of government and a basic duty to act if they are not.

This book is chock full of facts, figures, quotes, poll numbers, laws, and economic data but, to keep the subject matter accessible, it was necessary to streamline the work by omitting additional supporting evidence. This was especially true in relation to the legal and constitutional aspects of States leaving the Union and the original intent behind the construction of the United States.

For a more in-depth examination of the nature of the federal union, I recommend the book *A Brief Enquiry Into The True Nature and Character of Our Federal Government* by Abel Parker Upshur. I would also recommend that, if you want to take a deeper dive into the concepts and principles behind Texit, you can start by reading the reports or books specifically mentioned in this book in their entirety.

Throughout the book, you will see various capitalizations, punctuation, and grammar used that, at first glance, may seem inconsistent. In discussing the States of the United States, I use a capital 'S' whereas, in speaking of states in their general sense, I use the lowercase. This happens in all instances except when quoting some of the founding documents of the United States where their standards of punctuation have a direct bearing on the issues raised in this book. Also, in this book, the term United States is most often treated in its plural sense. The "United States are" was the clear intention at the founding of the Union, while "United States is" was a later usage adopted to reinforce a fallacy about the construction of the Union.

Additionally, in all instances where quotes are used, they are directly attributed within the text and I've provided enough information for readers to verify their accuracy by a simple Internet search.

Many of the concepts and issues raised in this book are neither new nor unique. This is, however, the first time all of them have been combined into a single work on the issue of Texas independence. I have not held back on slaughtering sacred cows and throwing their remains on a Texas-sized bar-b-que. Nor have I spared any politicians, especially those with whom I have had personal experience on this issue.

The critics will mercilessly attack this work because it is counter to the accepted political dogma of the day. History will judge this work, but the real judges as to its validity will be the people of Texas and all who seek the promise of self-determination. It is to them that I commit this work.

INTRODUCTION

> **"**Cowardice asks the question, 'Is it safe?' Expediency asks the question, 'Is it politic?' Vanity asks the question, 'Is it popular?' But, conscience asks the question, 'Is it right?' And there comes a time when one must take a position that is neither safe, nor politic, nor popular, but one must take it because one's conscience tells one that it is right.**"**
>
> *Martin Luther King, Jr.*

Until the last few years, Texit has not been a topic that is safe, politic, nor popular. But the belief by its most ardent supporters that it is right for Texas and Texans has been infectious. Spurred by the daily displays of federal dysfunction, Texans find their long-standing assumptions challenged by the questions that Texit poses, and compelled by the promise and hope that an independent Texas presents.

Texit is inevitable. It is no longer just a hope, wish, or dream. Rather, it is a statement of fact, a certainty in a world filled with so much uncertainty. It represents a fixed point in the future of Texas that is growing closer every day. However, it is what led us to this point, the journey getting there, and what lies beyond that has lacked explanation and clarity. To use a phrase popular with a previous generation of Texans, there are more questions than "Carter has liver pills."

In the 20 years I have spent working for an independent Texas, I have asked and been asked nearly every conceivable question about the issue. A staggering amount of research had to be done to get the right answers to these questions. The challenge, even to this day, is that answers have been hard to come by.

In a day and age where you can literally access the entire collected knowledge of mankind with a few keystrokes, answers about Texas independence can still prove elusive. The answers require research into a patchwork of subjects such as constitutional law, international law, treaties, geopolitical trends, voting patterns, polling data, government spending, economics, federal and state policy, history, and many other subjects too numerous to list.

The challenge was highlighted in recent years when two separate graduate students, who were each doing a thesis on the modern movement for Texas independence, contacted me. In the interviews, they lamented the difficulty of their task. Given the amount of discussion over the years, their expectation was that there was an abundance of scholarly work on the issue but, in their research, they found virtually nothing on the subject in academic journals. What they did find was a smattering of news articles that never dealt with the subject in depth, elected officials who didn't want to talk on the record, and the same three or four associate professors who had given definitive answers on the impossibility of Texit supported by vague rationale.

Their frustration was all too familiar. It has personally been an exercise in frustration for me for more than two decades. However, what has been most frustrating is arriving at truly well thought-out, well-researched answers, only to have them stifled by what amounts to a modern-day Spanish Inquisition. To utter the heresy that States of the United States can and should leave the Union will get you burned at the proverbial stake or excommunicated from public life.

While the mainstream media and the political establishment celebrate every conceivable opinion and lifestyle, Texas independence seems to be a no-go zone. Men can identify as women, women can identify as men, either can identify as nothing, Islamic terrorists can rampage across Europe and the Middle East, criminal gangs can ravage our border with Mexico, and illegal aliens can enter the country with impunity and demand to be taken in. All these issues have their cadre of supporters and apologists on both sides. Excuses and justifications for every act, lifestyle, and belief are given, debated, and accepted in every forum. Yet the moment a serious discussion begins about Texas leaving the Union, we are treated to incoherent rants about its criminality, its "inherent racism," and the pat and dismissive declaration of how it can "never happen."

The taboo seems to be exclusive to Texas, though. From the period of 1995 to the 2000 presidential election, any notion of Texas becoming an independent nation was classified as "domestic terrorism," "sedition," and "treason." Proponents, including me, were subjected to investigation and scrutiny by law enforcement, publicly ostracized, lost jobs or customers, and were the subject of libelous accusations and slurs in the media. However, in the aftermath of the highly contentious 2000 presidential election, secession suddenly gained popularity among those who had previously railed against it. However, not for Texas.

Their sudden change of heart was best reflected in a post-election piece in the *New York Times* by columnist Peter Applebome where he proclaimed:

"...if this domestic brawl cannot be amicably settled—and it's hard to see how that's possible—maybe it's time for the proper endgame not for bad elections but for bad marriages: divorce. Splitting the country into two would allow both Gov. George W. Bush and Vice President Al Gore to get to be president. The angry combatants would be pulled apart just like rowdy kids on the playground. And the two surly sides would be free to live in the two different countries they basically want to see."

Yet, when Barack Obama claimed the presidency in 2008, discussion of leaving the Union was again taboo. However taboo the subject may have become, it did little to curb support for the idea, which continued to grow in Texas. Largely ignored by the mainstream media and establishment politicians, support for Texas leaving the Union grew from single-digit polling under Clinton to 35 percent during Barack Obama's first term. The most recent polling in Texas shows that a majority of Republicans, approximately half of independent voters, and around one-third of Democrats support independence.

Then the Trump presidency happened. The newly formed movement of Californians who wanted independence was dubbed CalExit and became the darling of the left-leaning media. Tech entrepreneurs gave interviews touting the endless possibilities inherent in an independent California, and media outlets that had previously toed the "party line" of the indivisibility of the Union and ridiculed Texans who thought otherwise suddenly became the unofficial propaganda arm of the CalExit movement.

Even with the mainstream media's inconsistent opposition to a state leaving the Union off the table for now, support for an independent Texas is higher than ever, yet supporters cannot seem to break through to the next level. While the majority of Texans who support independence have been keen to show their support in anonymous polls or in ways they feel are safe, public shows of support have been a different matter altogether. Rallies on the issue suffer from poor attendance, financial contributions to pro-independence causes are lackluster, and elected officials will not speak publicly on the issue. The vast majority of supporters of Texas independence suffer from an inferiority complex, a crisis of conscience that would seem alien to the men and women who won the Texas Revolution in 1836.

There is, however, a core of support that continues to advocate and advance the cause. It is those ardent and zealous advocates who, perhaps channeling the spirit that won the Texas Revolution, have carried the banner for the rest. In the face of media bias, academic silence, and politicians who treat Texas independence as a convenient applause line, there have been breakthroughs.

In 2016, the Republican Party of Texas held its state convention. In an effort spearheaded by the Texas Nationalist Movement (TNM), a proposal that would have added a plank to the official platform calling for an up-or-down vote on Texas leaving the Union was considered. The proposal passed the Temporary Platform Committee by a two-thirds majority, throwing Party Chairman Tom Mechler and the staff of Governor Greg Abbott into an absolute panic. Defying all precedent, Mechler and the governor's agents lobbied to replace members of the Temporary Platform Committee with members who were opposed to the plank before the committee became the Permanent Platform Committee.

The unprecedented nature of the response from the political establishment cannot be overstated. One convention delegate, a longtime Republican activist said, "I've been coming to conventions for 30 years and I have never seen this."

In the ashes of this power play, the Permanent Platform Committee took up the platform passed by the Temporary Platform Committee. Immediately a motion was made to strike the call for an independence referendum from the platform. The motion passed by two votes. What is perhaps most telling about this is that the independence referendum language was the only proposed plank struck from the platform. This move was even more insidious and was indicative of the grand strategy of the establishment political machine. Passage of the platform by the Permanent Platform Committee was the passage of a proposed platform, not the platform in its final incarnation. Its next step was for the platform to be presented to the full convention where it would have been open to debate and a final vote. The committee and, by proxy, the establishment politicians, had effectively stifled any public debate or discussion on the issue of Texas independence. At least that's what they thought.

When the convention met in its capacity as a deliberative body to certify the new platform, the first person on the microphone was Regina Cowan. Cowan, a native of the small northeast Texas town of Beckville, now resides in the slightly larger city of Yorktown. Carried south by her husband's work in the oil field, Cowan is a mother, a small business owner, and an ardent supporter of Texas independence. She also happens to be the county chair for the Republican Party in Dewitt County.

In full view of Tom Mechler in his role as convention chair, 9,000 attendees, and media outlets from all over Texas and the United States, Cowan made a motion to add an even stronger plank, calling on the Republican Party of Texas to support, not just a vote on independence, but for actual, outright independence. It took two or three seconds for the convention to fully comprehend her motion. But, once it had properly sunk in, the convention erupted in applause, shouts, and cheers. It was, by far, the strongest positive reaction to anything that happened during the entire convention.

Imagine for a moment that you are Tom Mechler. Mechler, who closely resembles the cowboy from the Village People, doesn't seem like your typical political operative. Yet he considered the position of chair of the Republican Party of Texas his dream job. While the position is unpaid, it has a certain gravitas. The Republican Party of Texas is the largest state political party in the United States. Republicans hold all major statewide offices. Both chambers of the Texas Legislature have massive Republican majorities. Republicans hold the vast majority of county-level offices. As chairman, you get to hobnob with the state's top officials and get treated like royalty by the party faithful. You are the boss.

With the looming specter of a serious push within his party to call for an independence vote, Mechler was incredulous. "I don't anticipate them being successful at the state convention," he stated in one interview. "There is a lot of discussion on the part of a small group of people and they have a very loud voice," he added.

Mechler looked stunned. In Texas, we refer to that look as "getting hit in the face with a sock full of wet crap." That "small group" was actually a majority of the convention he was standing in front of. And the "very loud voice" was now amplified across Texas and the rest of the United States, thanks to the presence of the media.

Mechler did his best to maintain his composure during the ensuing floor debate, but the look on his face betrayed the fact that he couldn't fully comprehend what he was witnessing. What had been painted as a small fringe group by the opposition emerged as a cohesive movement that accurately reflected the sentiments of the dominant political party in Texas. One by one, the speakers in favor of adding the plank to the platform proceeded to destroy the common slurs about independence supporters and, in doing so, destroyed any credibility Mechler had on the issue.

Once the slur that independence is only supported by "old men" was destroyed by Cowan simply introducing the motion, the next speaker in favor of independence shattered some of the most persistent mischaracterizations of Texit supporters. After introducing the motion, Cowan yielded her speaking time to Alan Vera to make the first argument in favor of the motion.

Vera is well known in Texas political circles. He has been a vocal advocate for ballot integrity, serving in the Harris County Republican

Party as the head of election security, and he was one of the founders of True The Vote, which has fought for election integrity across the United States. His resume is impressive in business as well. He's a CEO, has served on the boards of several business organizations, and has worked with major corporations, all of which led to his nomination as Entrepreneur of the Year from the Houston Hispanic Chamber of Commerce. He served five years in the U.S. Army as an Airborne Ranger, attaining the rank of captain, where he received numerous individual and unit awards and citations. In addition, he is a Magna Cum Laude graduate of Loyola University in New Orleans, where he also received many academic, leadership and military honors, including Distinguished Military Graduate.

When Vera took to the mic and laid down one of the core reasons why support for Texas independence has grown, he received a standing ovation. His indictment that the federal government has buried "states' rights at the bottom of a landfill" was not the only reason people applauded. It was him. In front of everyone, a military officer from an elite unit, a recognized and successful Hispanic business owner, a known political operative, and a resident of one of the most populous cities in the world, declared without shame, reservation, or equivocation, his unapologetic support for Texit.

I can say with certainty that Mechler and others within the political establishment never expected any of this to happen. If they did, I am equally certain that it played out much differently in their heads. While the speakers in favor of the independence plank exuded confidence, credibility, and intelligence, the opposition was reduced to shrieking, incomprehensible tirades on how even the discussion of independence was treason and unpatriotic, which elicited laughter and jeers from the convention attendees.

When the time came for a vote, Mechler called for a voice vote.

The sound of the crowd was overwhelmingly in favor of adding the plank to the platform. To buy time, Mechler declared it "too close to call," prompting booing that was just as loud. He called for a standing vote, and the delegates made it clear that they chose to add it to the platform. Still, Mechler decisively declared that "the nays have it." This was a bridge too far for many of the delegates. After spending a week watching Mechler carry the water for the political establishment and his willingness to ignore the will of the body, a massive number of people walked out of the convention. As we say in Texas, "the horse was out of the barn." As David R. Brockman, reporting the convention for the left-leaning *Texas Observer*, put it, "Good God, I'm trapped in a room, surrounded by folks who just seriously considered the idea of secession."

Therein lies the problem. Even as earth-shattering as the floor fight was over a simple vote on Texas independence, it was still just a debate on whether independence should even be debated. While there have been public displays of support and some very public breakthroughs like the convention, in reality there still hasn't been a serious public discussion on the merits of Texas independence, the unbalanced relationship between the federal government and the States, the process necessary to obtain a referendum on independence, or what a post-exit Texas would look like.

The fact is that, in this political climate, it is nearly impossible to have a rational discussion about fundamental issues of governance in the absence of a deadline that serves as a pure expression of political will. Even then, having a rational discussion of this nature is akin to taking the twelve labors of Hercules, doubling the number, and increasing their difficulty by a factor of ten. However, it can be done and has been done successfully for decades.

At the end of the Second World War, there were 54 internationally recognized countries in the world. In 1973, the year of my birth, that number had grown to approximately 120. At the end of the 20th century, there were 192. As of 2017, the official number is 195, with at least two dozen or more in the process of seeking international recognition. There are no fewer than 100 other movements in the world seeking exit from their current country or working to leave larger political unions.

There are plenty of examples to show that both the debate on independence, as well as actual independence, can happen. The knowledge and information, although hard to come by, exists to support the claims by Texit advocates. There is a clear legal basis to determine the path and process under which Texit could happen. There is a willingness and desire by more than enough Texans to have a serious debate on the issue that culminates in an up-or-down vote by the people of Texas. And, with utmost certainty, there is a spirit of independence within the people of Texas that will lead them to embrace Texit, lift their heads, and stand among the nations.

1 | WHAT IS TEXIT?

66 Texas will again lift its head and stand among the nations. It ought to do so, for no country upon the globe can compare with it in natural advantages. 99

Sam Houston

In 2012, the Eurozone—a term used to describe the nations of the European Union who use a single currency—began to publicly show the first signs of an existential crisis. With the economy of Greece in shambles and the Greek people having difficulty forming a government, speculation mounted that Greece would pull out of the Eurozone, drop the Euro as its currency, and re-adopt the drachma.

Economists further speculated that, if Greece chose to leave the Eurozone, it would also seek withdrawal from the European Union altogether. Some speculated that, even if Greece didn't choose to fully leave the European Union, the financial shockwave that would be created in other EU states by its rejection of the Euro would prompt other members to expel them.

In an effort to simplify the language surrounding the issue of Greece's potential departure from the Eurozone, two economists from Citigroup, Ebrahim Rahbari and William H. Butler, began using a mash-up of "Greece" and "exit." The term "Grexit" was born.

The use of Grexit was generally reserved for the political establishment, EU policy wonks and economists, and never found fertile ground in the minds of the public. While the Greeks may have given birth to western civilization, it took the British, in common British fashion, to spread the "exit" mash-up to the rest of the world.

Lamenting the Greek Eurozone crisis and the rise of voices in the United Kingdom that were resisting further economic and political integration with the European Union, blogger Peter Wilding wrote:

"Unless a clear view is pushed that Britain must lead in Europe at the very least to achieve the completion of the single market then the portmanteau for Greek euro exit might be followed by another sad word, Brexit."

The term "Brexit" spread quickly and was picked up by the leading proponents of Britain's exit from the European Union. Leader of the U.K. Independence Party, Nigel Farage, and others within the party began to use the term frequently in speeches and in the media. Pro-Brexit members of the Conservative and Labour Parties picked it up. The opposition began to rail against "Brexit" and the public began infusing their discussions on the European Union with the term.

As Prime Minister David Cameron called for a referendum on Britain's membership in the European Union, it wasn't too long before a connection was made between the term Brexit and Texas' very own, long-gestating movement for independence. In the wake of the results of the Brexit referendum, domestic media turned its eye toward Texas and began asking the question, "Is Texit next?"

Understandably, a Texas exit has been on the radar for many years. In fact, many people still wonder why Texas hasn't exited already.

THE FACE OF TEXIT

In 2009, Research 2000 conducted a poll of Texans and asked them this question: "Do you think Texas would be better off as an independent nation or as part of the United States of America?"

The results were trumpeted to the media and parroted by numerous media outlets. "Only 35% of the 600 Texans surveyed believed that Texas would be better off as an independent nation." However, the left-leaning *Burnt Orange Report* did something that most media outlets did not. They looked at the actual results and caught something that no other outlet bothered to check.

"The Research 2000 Texas Poll was conducted from April 20 through April 22, 2009. A total of 600 likely voters who vote regularly in state elections were interviewed statewide by telephone. The poll was 39% Republican, 33% Democrat, and 28% independent."

Looking at the breakdown by political affiliation changed the landscape. Forty-eight percent of Republicans, 40 percent of independent voters, and 15 percent of Democrats believed that Texans would benefit from independence. The numerical breakdown matters, especially in a state where Republicans have a lock on every statewide office and where independents claim their electoral independence but typically vote for Republican candidates.

The percentages broken down by political affiliation weren't the only earth-shattering information in the poll. Also buried in that statement was the real key to unlocking the real impact of the survey. The respondents were likely voters who also regularly voted.

However, one poll does not make a trend. In 2014, a Reuters/IPSOS poll asked a slightly different question. Rather than asking a question about whether Texans felt they *would* be better off under the flag of independence, respondents were asked if they felt Texas *should* leave the Union. The difference between the two questions is very important. The Research 2000 poll was a question about perceived benefit. The Reuters/IPSOS question was a question of political will. The results, again broken down by political affiliation, showed 54 percent of Republicans, 49 percent of independent voters, and 35 percent of Democrats favored an independent Texas.

While the political trend obvious in these two polls is the growth of support for Texit and the strengthening of the attitudes of the voters, what goes virtually unnoticed by pundits is what these numbers look like in reality. When these percentages are overlaid with the actual voting patterns of Texans in statewide races, support for Texit, on average, polls anywhere from 6 to 10 percentage points higher than those who want to stay in the Union.

However startling that fact may be, the more important story might be who is supporting Texit beyond political affiliation. Those who are opposed to Texit have largely been the ones who have painted the public portrait of the "typical" Texit supporter. In their minds, and reinforced by the media, Texit supporters are poor, uneducated, rural white men over 60, Fox News fanatics that are anti-American to the point of making the Islamic State look like fans of Toby Keith, baseball, and apple pie.

This imagery was rather effective at keeping the vast majority of Texit supporters "in the closet" and politically inert on the issue for many years. The implication was that, if you supported Texit but didn't look like this caricature of the average Texit supporter, you were an outlier. However, as the real face of Texit has begun to emerge over the past several years, the opposition's portrayal has started to crumble.

One of the first indicators that support for Texit was something different than it was often portrayed came in the aforementioned Reuters/IPSOS poll when 35 percent of Democrats favored independence. The Democratic Party publicly promotes itself as racially diverse, gender inclusive, and young, all traits that no pundit has ever ascribed to Texit supporters. Therefore, one would expect that number to be zero percent. It wasn't.

Acknowledging the disconnect between the public portrayal of Texit support and the real-life interactions occurring with Texit supporters, the TNM conducted its own internal survey in 2015. In the largest Texit survey ever conducted, the TNM, asking a battery of questions, polled 10,000 Texas voters who support Texit. The results represent the clearest picture of Texit supporters to date.

According to the survey, 35 percent of the respondents are active duty military, reserve military, members of the Texas State Guard, or veterans. Included in this number were veterans from every military conflict since, and including, the Second World War. The military supporters of Texit cited three specific reasons for their support: the oath they took to support, protect, and defend a Constitution they felt has been ignored by the federal government; their sense of betrayal by the federal government for their service; and their love of Texas. To them, their love of America was a love of the principles on which this country was founded and not blind obedience to a government that, in their minds, was ignoring those principles.

That same survey showed that 96 percent of Texit supporters are employed or self-employed, with 33 percent earning $50-$75k annually. They are also well educated, with 74 percent being college educated and 7 percent holding masters' or doctoral degrees. In addition, while the percentages of supporters per capita was significant in the rural areas of Texas, the highest concentrations of supporters were found in the major metropolitan areas of Houston, San Antonio, and Dallas.

Contrary to the established narrative, Texit supporters proved to be educated, productive, stable, and well dispersed throughout Texas, including politically coveted, highly populated urban centers. Many honorably served in the United States military to protect and defend the principles of a federative constitutional republic and, while saluting the fifty-starred flag, never forgot that the 28th star was theirs to reclaim at will.

Texit supporters are also destroying the "old and white" stereotype. The impending "demographic shift" that some analysts predict will "turn Texas blue" might, in fact, turn Texas into an independent nation.

A February 2014 University of Texas/Texas Tribune Poll asked respondents whether they considered themselves Texans first and Americans second, or Americans first and Texans second. The results point in an interesting direction, where the largest ethnic group identifying as Texans first was not Anglos, "but are instead the growing population of Hispanics, among whom 33 percent identify as Texan first."

To those opposed to Texit, that result must have come as a shock. But any hope they might have had that the issue would die with its "old" supporters was also dashed by one of the other facts brought to light in the *Texas Tribune's* announcement of the results.

"Maybe even more surprising, younger voters are more inclined to call themselves Texans first. A slight majority of those who identify as Texans first are between the ages of 18 and 44 years old. Among 18- to 29-year-olds, 40 percent identify as Texans before they identify as Americans, far outpacing any other age group."

This strength of support among Texas youth was highlighted at the 2017 meeting of Texas Boys State. Created in 1935, Boys State is a summer leadership program of the American Legion, specifically geared toward high school juniors. Since its inception, it has been the launching pad for kids who go on to become political heavyweights. Past participants have included well-known names such as founder and former CEO of Fox News Roger Ailes, Supreme Court Justice Samuel Alito, Vice President Dick Cheney, New Jersey Governor Chris Christie, President Bill Clinton, Governor Mike Huckabee, radio host Rush Limbaugh, and many others.

In each State, participants are divided into two mock political parties, the Nationalists and the Federalists. They conduct a mock legislative session where each house proposes legislation, debates it, and votes on it. In all respects, it follows the legislative process in the State where it is held.

In 2017, Texas Boys State made headlines when a bill calling for Texas to leave the Union was introduced and passed both houses. One of the participants shot video of the final vote. As the results were announced, the gallery erupted in thunderous applause. The headlines the next day were full of media skepticism and indignance. But there were those who understood that this generation of Boys State participants are destined to become the political leaders of tomorrow and, among them, indignance was nowhere to be found.

It seems that the conclusion drawn by the *Texas Tribune* to its poll results three years earlier was confirmed.

"It's not grandpa that places the Lone Star over the Stars and Stripes, but his grandchildren."

While surveys and polling data inject a certain authority into identifying the real face of Texit, what Texans understand on the matter comes from their individual experiences. Texit supporters are as diverse as Texas. Everyone in Texas personally knows a Texit supporter. Every Texan lives in a neighborhood with other Texit supporters. Every Texan either works with or employs one or more Texit supporters. That person who just served your food at a restaurant is just as likely to be a Texit supporter as is the person who owns the restaurant. The person sitting beside you in traffic, the parents of your child's classmates, or even your children themselves are equally likely to be Texit supporters. The face of Texit could be sitting right next to you.

THE HISTORY AND CULTURE OF TEXIT

Few outside of Texas understand how ingrained the mindset of independence is in the collective consciousness of Texans. Even some within Texas struggle to understand it. Most Texans just call it "being a Texan." However, the historical and cultural roots of Texit are real and run deep.

If you want to gauge the importance placed on the history of Texas by Texans, just ask any child who has completed 7th grade in a Texas public school, where completion of a course specifically on the history of Texas is mandatory. It's not taught as a unit of U.S. history nor does it simply occupy a couple of chapters in a textbook. It stands, like Texas itself, separate and distinct from the history of the rest of the United States.

In the Texas History course, children are taught that Texas was a wilderness, harsh and formidable, yet bountiful. It was rugged, wild, and dangerous and could only be tamed by a people as rugged, wild, and dangerous as the land itself. Even when the globe-spanning empires of France and Spain alternately occupied Texas, they never really possessed it. Scattered outposts and missions gave way to settlers from around the world when it became a state of Mexico. The message was clear to prospective settlers. If they were tough and independent enough, they could carve out a home they could call their own.

Those settlers mainly came from the States of the fledgling United States. Many of them, driven by personal and professional failures in the land of their birth, sought a clean slate and a second chance in Tejas. Joining those Tejanos who had already called it home for generations, they built small communities and worked together to carve out their own piece of heaven. Only one generation removed from the American Revolution, these settlers also brought with them an uncompromising worldview on the inherent rights of the individual and the role and function of the government in a federative republic. They also brought a virulent hatred of tyranny.

The government in Mexico City was overthrown in what amounted to a military coup and the constitution under which Mexico was governed was suspended. The people of the Mexican States rose up, none more so than the inhabitants of Tejas. Recalling the stand taken by the American colonists against the actions of the king of England, Texans defied the actions of dictator Santa Anna.

When Santa Anna ordered Mexican troops to seize a small cannon held in the town of Gonzales, the Texans refused to surrender it. Instead, they hoisted a defiant white banner with a crude representation of the cannon, a single star, and the English version of words, spoken more than 2,000 years prior by the Spartan king Leonidas to the Persian emperor Xerxes when he made a similar demand: "COME AND TAKE IT."

The Texans held on to their cannon in the small skirmish that would later be known as the first battle of the Texas Revolution, but Texans were still divided on what the response to the unconstitutional acts of the Mexican government should be. Many, seeing Santa Anna's actions through Mexico, viewed them as a declaration of war against the people. Santa Anna pursued a strategy that could be defined, at best, as a "war of extermination" and, if committed today, would be classified as a war crime. A letter, penned by the hastily formed Committee of Safety in the aptly named town of Liberty, highlights the divide of the day.

The committee of safety for the municipality of Liberty, in the exercise of the functions delegated to them, feel it their duty to address their fellow-citizens of the municipality, on the present interesting nature of our public affairs.

The committee are sensible that many worthy and patriotic citizens have been opposed, on principles which they esteemed sound and correct, to a rupture with the authorities of Mexico. The committee know how to appreciate such opposition and the motives from which it proceeds.

But they would earnestly solicit such as still adhere to an opposition which may have been innocent, and even praise-worthy in its origin, to reconsider the subject, and to inquire whether the present situation of the country does not essentially change the ground on which their opposition was predicated. The committee are free to declare that they, too, were advocates for peace, while peace was practicable on terms compatible with the welfare, the honor, and the future safety of Texas, and of the constitution which we have all sworn to support and obey. The hope of such a peace has departed, without leaving a single ray of light to guide the most credulous in the indulgence of it. We, therefore, call upon all such, to abandon an opposition which, however commendable in its origin, can now have no application to the circumstances of the country. Right principles never change; but, in the application of principles to facts, there are many modifications. The federal constitution and the constitution of the states have been violently destroyed, and the actual powers of the government are usurped by the military, who are exercising them with the wonted cruelty and recklessness of the rights of citizens that has always characterized the dominion of the sword.

Of those of our fellow-citizens who regard the sanctity of their oaths of allegiance and allege it as a reason for opposing their countrymen now in arms, we would enquire what is the obligation of that oath? Most clearly, it is to support the federal and state constitution. But where are those constitutions? They have been rent to atoms, and their scattered fragments are to be traced, in lines of blood, beneath the trampling of the usurper's cavalry, on the plains of Zacatecas.

Texas is but pursuing the noble, unsuccessful example of that high minded state. She has resolved to sustain a legitimate government, or to perish in the attempt; to oppose the tide of military and ecclesiastical usurpation, and to roll it back upon the unholy league. And she looks with confidence for the aid of her adjacent sister states, who have already experienced the bitterness of military misrule. For this purpose the sword is already drawn; our fellow-citizens are in the field, the banner of liberty is unfolded, and the high example of lawful resistance to unlawful usurpation is exhibited in the gleam of their rifles and the thunder of their cannon, before the walls of San Antonio.

The committee would, therefore, affectionately appeal to such of their fellow-citizens as are still holding back from the good work, in the language of the holy prophet, 'Why halt ye between two opinions?' If the constitution be the object of your allegiance, then rise up, like men, and support the constitution. If Santa Anna and his military vassals be the government you desire, then avow yourselves the degraded minions of an unprincipled and infuriated despotism. The contest is for liberty or slavery; for life or death; for the tranquil possession of the country we have redeemed from barbarism, or a forcible ejectment from it. It admits of no neutrals.

Those who are not for us are against us. Those who refuse to save the country cannot hope to participate in the benefits of its salvation. Our numbers are few, but they are a band of heroes, and fear not the issue. Union is always important. The concurrence of every citizen is desirable. The few who still maintain their opposition are not dreaded; their number is small, their influence insignificant. But 'Texas expects every man to do his duty.'

The door of conciliation is open, and all are invited to enter. They will be received with cordiality, the past forgotten, and the future only will be regarded. The times are critical, the emergency is pressing, and calls for promptitude and energy. Texas is at war; and every citizen who shall be found in practices inimical to her interests will be dealt with according to the utmost rigor of military law.

The committee urge these things, not in the spirit of dictation, but of friendly admonition; not to alarm, but to convince and to allure every misguided citizen into the path of duty, of interest, and of honor. The aged and the infirm who cannot take the field can contribute of their substance; the young, the robust, and the gallant, are exhorted to repair to the camp, to unite with their brethren in arms, and to exhibit themselves the worthy descendants of the heroes of 76. Horses, arms, and ammunition are wanted, steady hands and brave hearts are wanted to repel the storm of desolation that lowers over our beautiful country. Let no man hold back too long; there is danger in delay: there is mischief in disunion: there is safety, happiness, and a speedy peace in a united, prompt, and decisive exertion of our strength. The committee would repeat the motto of the gallant hero of Trafalgar, 'Texas expects every man to do his duty.'

From that first skirmish came the first Battle of Bexar, where the now-christened Texians ran the Mexican army out of San Antonio, eventually leading to what is unarguably the most iconic moment in the Texas Revolution—the siege of the Alamo. The Mexican army offered surrender to the Alamo defenders, and 27-year-old commander of the Alamo William Barret Travis' response was a single defiant cannon shot. After 12 long days of siege by the numerically superior Mexican forces, legend says that Travis offered escape to those defenders who did not want to stay with him and face certain death, calling the question on his offer with a literal line in the sand drawn with his sword. Mere hours later, all the defenders lay dead on the grounds of the mission, never knowing that, four days earlier, a convention of delegates from all over Texas had drawn up and signed a Declaration of Independence from Mexico, formally establishing the Republic of Texas.

At the same time, Sam Houston, a former congressman and governor from Tennessee, had been tasked with building the Texian Army as its commanding general to defend the newly declared Republic from the forces of Santa Anna. There were few actual soldiers and even fewer actual supplies. Each volunteer brought his own rifle, his own provisions, and his uniform was the civilian dress of the day. There was no pay other than the promise of land for everyone who served, and that only if they won. Discipline was hard to maintain under these circumstances, but Houston managed to hold his ragtag army together in an eastward retreat until the right circumstances occurred. On April 21, 1836, on the low sloping plain of San Jacinto, the opportunity presented itself. Houston ordered a decisive do-or-die attack on the Mexican Army. Eighteen minutes later, the battle was over. A day later, Santa Anna was captured and a few weeks later, the Treaty of Velasco was signed. Texas was independent.

For nine brief years, Texas stood as a nation among nations. It had presidents, a congress, a supreme court, its own army, executed international treaties, and opened the door to trade and new settlers from all over the world. However, the debt accumulated during the war with Mexico and through the process of building a national infrastructure was a significant problem for the fledgling Republic. In hopes that joining the United States would help alleviate the burden brought on by the debt, the Texians applied to join.

The United States initially turned Texas away, fearing it would bring on a war with Mexico. The fear of a closer relationship between the independent Republic of Texas and Great Britain overrode the American fear of war with Mexico, and Texas was admitted into the Union by a Joint Resolution of Congress. However, Texans soon found out that the federal government stipulated that Texas would receive no help with its debts and, within months, the United States was at war with Mexico.

By the late 1840s, the State of Texas and the rest of the United States had come perilously close to military action against one another over the far western sections of Texas. To prevent Texas declaring independence twice in 20 years, an agreement was struck to pay Texas for ceding portions of its western and northwestern lands.

This is by no means a comprehensive history of Texas nor does it include the nuances and richness that are part of the Texas story. It is, though, one of the most critical periods of Texas history, and knowing it as the people of Texas know it, is key to understanding the historical roots of the modern-day Texit movement.

Texan self-sufficiency is found in the lives of those who tamed a wilderness. Texan defiance is found in the "Come and Take It" flag and Travis' cannon shot. Texan resistance to overreaching government finds its roots in the reactions of those first-generation Texians to actions of both the Mexican and American governments in those early days. Texans perceive their special status among the States from having been an independent republic, forged in fire and steel, and written in the blood of those who perished at the Alamo. Texans remember those who perished at Goliad as a warning that the price of surrender is often higher than the sacrifice of honor.

There is no doubt that this history of revolution, rebellion, and resistance in Texas plays an enormous role in the modern-day movement for independence. But history alone is not enough to fuel a modern, growing political movement.

In Texas, history and culture exist in a symbiotic relationship. More than any other State in the Union, Texas history has had a definitive, quantifiable impact on the development of its unique culture. In turn, the culture of Texas has led Texans to take bold, extraordinary acts that then become a part of the historical fabric. The cycle then repeats.

The federal government adopted a Pledge of Allegiance. Not to be outdone, the Texas Legislature created a Texas Pledge in 1933. In its current form, it states, "Honor the Texas flag; I pledge allegiance to thee, Texas, one state under God, one and indivisible." By law it must be recited by public school students between the U.S. pledge and a moment of silence.

The Texan struggle to maintain a national identity doesn't stop there. The *Star-Spangled Banner* was adopted as the American national anthem in 1931. Texas adopted *Texas, Our Texas* as the state song, the de facto national anthem of Texas, in 1929. The height of the Washington Monument is 555 feet. The height of the San Jacinto Monument, commemorating the victory of the Texian Army in the Texas Revolution, is 570 feet. The height of the United States Capitol Building is 289 feet. The height of the Texas Capitol Building is 308 feet.

This historical and cultural nationalism has manifested in other ways. Texas has turned its very shape into a symbol of pride. In grocery stores throughout Texas, you can find tortilla chips, waffle irons, and a number of other products in the shape of Texas. You can find Texas agricultural products clearly marked as "Texan" to differentiate from products that are from "elsewhere."

This has all served as a backdrop to threats of leaving the Union over the years. Whether it's the "Drive 80 Freeze A Yankee" bumper stickers in the 1970s or their modern-day equivalent, "SECEDE" stickers, the idea that Texas could break away and forge its own path has been a constant companion since the days of the Republic. So much so that it has become a staple of modern fiction.

Prior to the 1980s, the idea of Texit was almost nonexistent in fiction. That changed with the 1979 novel *The Power Exchange* by Alan R. Erwin that posits Texas leaving the Union in the wake of the federal energy crisis. *The Ayes of Texas*, a 1982 novel by Daniel Da Cruz, has Texas leaving the Union, spurred by an unholy treaty arrangement between the United States and the Soviet Union where the federal government cedes the entirety of its manufacturing base to the Soviets. The 2000s witnessed an explosion of Texit fiction, not only in print, but in all media.

An independent Republic of Texas played a major role in the 2005 video game Shattered Union. In Jericho, a 2006 TV series about the aftermath of a nuclear attack on the United States, the post-attack Independent Republic of Texas enters the story, coming to the aid of the protagonists and defending the principles of limited government and liberty against two aggressive factions seeking to remake the United States in their own image. These have been joined by additional, highly successful fictional novelizations like *Lone Star Daybreak* from Erik L. Larson and the *Patriots of Treason* series from David Thomas Roberts.

In 2017, Texit made the jump to the big screen in the movie *Bushwick*. The plot follows a pair of Brooklynites fleeing for their lives when a paramilitary army descends upon their neighborhood. The invasion is inexplicably sparked by Texas seceding from the Union.

If something can be described as being "as American as apple pie," it seems wholly appropriate to describe something as being "as Texan as Texit." Texans view Texas as something different, special, and set apart. The unspoken attitude produced by our history and embedded in our culture is that the Union is hanging onto Texas by a thread and we're holding a pair of scissors.

THE CENTURY OF SELF-DETERMINATION

It is important to recognize that the modern movement for Texas independence is not unique in a general sense and doesn't exist as some political or social aberration. In geopolitical circles, the 20th century is often referred to as the "American Century" in reference to the ascendency of the United States as a global power. However, in retrospect, the 20th century deserves a moniker that is more reflective of geopolitical reality—the Century of Self-Determination.

This reality was not lost on author John Naisbitt in his 1994 work *Global Paradox*. A product of Harvard and Cornell Universities who served in the Kennedy and Johnson administrations, Naisbitt dedicated his professional life to political and economic futurism. Analyzing economic trends led him to publish his breakthrough work, *Megatrends,* in 1982. It has since sold 14 million copies. He gained an amazing reputation for his accuracy in trends analysis, which led to other books and numerous academic honors.

Global Paradox was something different, though. While ostensibly a book on the impact of the telecommunications revolution on the world economy and how it was reshaping the future of global commerce, Naisbitt identified that the trend had political implications as well.

"The world's trends point overwhelmingly toward political independence and self-rule on one hand, and the formation of economic alliances on the other."

To be fair, Naisbitt didn't have to be a very good futurist to figure out the political ramifications of the trend. It was evident to anyone who had been paying moderate attention to world events since the end of the Second World War. Between the end of the war and the publication of *Global Paradox*, the number of countries in the world had nearly quadrupled and showed no signs of slowing down. Indeed, between the publication of *Megatrends* and *Global Paradox*, the world witnessed one of the most stunning displays of the collapse of a political and economic union when the Iron Curtain fell and the first members of the Soviet Union declared their independence. Those countries were not the larger states of the Union of Soviet Socialist Republics. They were, in fact, the three small Baltic states of Estonia, Latvia, and Lithuania.

Although the Bolshevik government renounced all claims to these three countries in 1920 as part of the Molotov-Ribbentrop Pact in 1939, Estonia and Latvia were declared part of the Soviet "sphere of influence," while Lithuania was handed over to the Germans. By 1940, all three came under armed occupation by Soviet troops, their governments removed and replaced with pro-Soviet administrators whose first act was to join the USSR.

By 1941, the Germans occupied all three countries until they were driven out by the Soviet invasion in 1944. In the post-war period, the Baltic states were considered full constituent republics of the Soviet Union that went on to declare their annexation of the territory as fully legal.

In 1989, as the Berlin Wall fell, the Baltic states made their move. They amended their own constitutions, declaring the supremacy of their own laws over the edicts flowing from Moscow. By 1991, they had made clear their intention to declare independence and, after unsuccessful attempts to overthrow their respective governments, these three small republics made good on their promise. For the first time in 50 years, the peoples of Latvia, Lithuania, and Estonia enjoyed the right of self-government.

Their bravery and tenacity proved to be the thread that, once tugged, unraveled a world power. By Christmas Day of 1991, 12 more members of the Soviet Union were independent, adding 15 new self-governing nations to the world in less than two years. In typical, succinct Russian fashion, Yevgeny Roizman, historian and mayor of Russia's third-largest city, Yekaterinburg, summed it up best when he said, "The Soviet Union broke up without a civil war, thank God."

While these dramatic events may have been a major factor that spurred Naisbitt to make the political connection with his economic trends forecast in *Global Paradox*, it is unlikely that they were the only thing. Self-determination was the single dominant factor in international relations in the 20th century.

Both World Wars were driven by imperialist claims to dominion over a variety of people and were fueled by dreams of territorial conquest. However, they were defined by the resistance to those aims and support for the right of people to determine how and by whom they would be governed. The battlefields of Europe, Asia, and Africa are soaked with the blood of tens of millions of soldiers who fought and died to defend the right of self-determination. Sometimes it was their own self-determination. More often than not, it was for the right of self-determination for someone else.

The devastation wrought was such that the countries of the world—before, during and after—struggled to come to grips with every aspect of self-determination and to create a framework under which people that wanted to govern themselves had the opportunity to do so without bloodshed.

While self-determination came into its own in the 20th century, its roots go back into antiquity. Since the dawn of civilization, tribes and nations have resisted outside governance. Throughout history, wherever you find an empire, you find resistance to its domination. However, the modern expression for a conscious self-determination can be traced back directly to the American Revolution. The writings and actions of those who are considered the Founding Fathers, inspired by John Locke and Thomas Hobbes, laid the groundwork for modern political thought on the matter. The case for self-determination is discussed in the writings of the day and succinctly described in the official documents of the era. You find the core principle of self-determination enshrined in the Declaration of Independence of the 13 colonies and the later Texas Declaration of Independence, which is this: governments govern only by consent of the governed.

As the New Imperialism swept across the world in the 19th century, people around the world, either consciously or unconsciously, embraced the core principle of the American Revolution. Much as it was in antiquity, so it was into the early 20th century. Empires grasped their possessions ever tighter. Yet the tighter their grip, the more the desire for self-determination flourished. Monarchies fell, empires weakened, and nations began to reassert their independence.

Governments around the world had to come to grips with the changing political landscape and the new geopolitical realities. After the United States' brief flirtation with overseas empire building in the late 1800s, President Woodrow Wilson kicked off the global discussion on self-determination when he issued his famous Fourteen Points. In an attempt to end the First World War and prevent future global conflicts, Wilson laid out a plan that he believed would ensure peace. The majority of the fourteen items were specific to the war and were meant to be terms of a peace treaty at the end of the war. Embedded in each of the items were subtle calls for respecting the right of self-determination for the people in the areas affected by the war. His final point, however, was not so subtle.

"A general association of nations must be formed under specific covenants for the purpose of affording mutual guarantees of political independence and territorial integrity to great and small states alike."

To clarify and reinforce his call for self-determination, Wilson gave a speech to a joint session of Congress in February of 1918. In the speech, he was very clear as to what he felt was the key underlying reason for the war.

"This war had its roots in the disregard of the rights of small nations and of nationalities which lacked the union and the force to make good their claim to determine their own allegiances and their own forms of political life."

Wilson, perhaps channeling Thomas Jefferson, issued a caution for those governments that fail to respect the right of self-determination.

"National aspirations must be respected; peoples may now be dominated and governed only by their own consent. 'Self-determination' is not a mere phrase. It is an imperative principle of action which statesmen will henceforth ignore at their peril."

After 18 million died in World War 1, the winning side still chose to ignore Wilson's warning. The Treaty of Versailles that ended the war relied more on a thirst for retribution than an acknowledgement of the true causes of the war, and relegated the issues of self-determination, raised by Wilson, to the back burner. In 1945, the peril warned of by Wilson would be counted in the 60 to 80 million lives lost in the Second World War.

Reeling from the loss of a full three percent of the world's population, the global community began to seriously and consciously contemplate self-determination. As the post-war Iron Curtain of communism descended over Europe, it seemed that the lessons learned from two world wars would be ignored yet again. They weren't, but it took some time for them to be implemented.

The first major international attempt to enshrine self-determination as an acknowledged and fundamental right of nations and people came in the charter of the United Nations. For all of its failings and weaknesses, there was at least an attempt to place self-determination in the forefront of geopolitical thought, if not entirely in practice.

"To develop friendly relations among nations based on respect for the principle of equal rights and self-determination of peoples."

These words are found in Article 1, Section 2 of the United Nations Charter and serve as one of the stated purposes of the organization. It is these words that have guided the international community in support of self-determination around the world ever since.

At the founding of the United Nations in 1945, 750 million people—nearly one-third of the world's population—lived under the authority of another power and did not enjoy the right of self-government. The conscious implementation of the principle of self-determination was the driving force behind a decades-long international effort of decolonization. Today, that number is approximately 2 million.

The success of decolonization inspired other nations who were fully incorporated into other countries or were members of a larger political and economic union to reevaluate their individual situations and choose independence. The effect was nothing less than miraculous. People who were told their entire lives that they were incapable of self-government found themselves masters of their own destiny. No matter the size, no matter the perceived difficulties, they became nations that stood shoulder to shoulder with those who had once held them in check.

GLOBAL EXIT IN THE 21ST CENTURY

Naisbitt identified the trend in 1994. The right of self-determination was gaining clarity and converts who were willing to embrace it. However, larger western powers, who thought they were immune to its effects close to their centers of power, entered the 21st century in a state of denial about the power, scope, and inspirational potential of self-determination.

The two collections of peoples who were, and still are, in the deepest denial were both born of self-determination in response to imperial overreach. They purport to be the biggest champions of the right of peoples around the world to self-government, and each has used military force in support of independence in every corner of the world, shedding precious blood in its defense. These two are none other than Europe and the United States.

If there was any thought that Europe and the United States would somehow buck the global trend toward self-determination, the Brexit vote in June 2016 put an end to that speculation. In the minds of Texit advocates, and advocates of other independence movements, the real story was that voters in a First World country had gone to the ballot box and chosen to separate from a bloated, bureaucratic political and economic union that was becoming more centralized and authoritarian in its drive toward a more perfect union. In short, if the United Kingdom can reclaim its sovereignty and right of self-government, anyone can.

Brexit has sparked a renewed drive toward a second Scottish referendum and given hope to scores of other Eurosceptic movements on the continent that have been questioning their relationship within the European Union for years. Its effects have been felt in the United States as well. By adding one key element to the debate—hope—it has had a dramatic effect in Texas as well as New Hampshire, Vermont, and California. It is spurring conversations and political action, and encouraging people in the States to fundamentally reexamine their State's place within the Union.

The movements of the 21st century are fueled less by old grievances over territory and more by pragmatic issues of economics and self-governance. The idea that the people of a nation-state must give up the right of self-government and identity as part of a larger union or country to adequately address trade or national security concerns is becoming increasingly anachronistic in this century.

This realization is responsible for fueling more independence movements than ever around the world. For every movement that grabs the attention of the United States, there are far more that do not. These movements, however, show the universality of the desire for self-determination and self-government.

Our neighbor to the north, Canada, is home to several independence movements in various states of organization. There is the well-known and politically successful Parti Quebecois in Quebec that has forced multiple referenda on independence. There is the Alberta Independence Movement that is at the forefront of a movement to lead all of the western provinces from under the thumb of Ottawa. There are also scattered movements within the Atlantic Provinces in Eastern Canada.

Canada's proximity to the United States and the discussions of independence in both has led to some interesting propositions. The late Dr. Thomas Naylor of the Second Vermont Republic proposed a confederation of Vermont, New Hampshire, Maine, and the Atlantic provinces of Canada that would be the North American equivalent of Denmark. Similarly, there have been discussions about Oregon and Washington exiting the Union and joining with British Columbia in a Pacific Northwest confederation of these politically and socially aligned territories.

Even to our south, we find self-determination rearing its head among those who were once considered the compatriots of Texans. There have been rumblings over the past decade of legitimate political movements organizing to have the northern states of Mexico leave and declare independence, resurrecting the idea of a Republic of the Rio Grande. Their grievances sound like those espoused by Texit advocates. They are tired of their developing industries serving as the cash cow for the less productive parts of Mexico. They are tired of illegal immigrants from Central America using their states as the jumping-off point for entry into Texas and the United States. They are tired of the lawlessness and violence of the cartels and the impotence or unwillingness of the Mexican Federales to put a stop to it.

The central government in Mexico City is nervous enough about the possibility of a Republic of the Rio Grande that there have been proposals in recent years to change the official name of the country simply to Mexico from Estados Unidos Mexicanos, which translates into United Mexican States, for fear that the name alone might bolster support for greater state sovereignty and outright independence.

Even farther south, we see a flourishing independence movement in Sao Paulo, Brazil. The Movimento Sao Paulo Independente (MSPI) has been successful in taking their case to the people of Sao Paulo with messaging that should seem quite familiar. They believe the Brazilian central bureaucracy is too large and too inefficient. They advocate for lower taxes, decentralization of power, restoration of family values, and protection of the distinctiveness of their culture.

Across the Atlantic in Africa, we are seeing self-determination raise its head under one of the most repressive regimes on the continent. The Matabeleland Liberation Organisation is waging a peaceful fight to liberate its homeland from the clutches of the brutal dictatorship of Robert Mugabe and his successors. Their leader, Paul Siwela, is under constant threat of arrest and Mugabe loyalists have not been shy in their application of violence. However, Siwela and his allies persist in the face of threats of violence and accusations of treason.

One of the biggest factors in the growth of independence movements in the 21st century has been the spread of globalism. Globalism seeks total economic integration across the planet. It is, at its core, Soviet-style central economic planning on an unprecedented scale. The effects of globalism have created poverty, unrest, and destruction around the world as the global elite seek to remake the world in their image.

Globalists, often public proponents of self-determination, harbor a deep-seated contempt for it. In their minds, self-determination, secession, and nationalism walk hand in hand, and all three are the true threat to the global elite's brand of globalism. Their brand of globalism views nation-states, and all they entail, as impediments to their dreams of a truly integrated world. In their world, borders, identities, and self-interests take a backseat to their true driving forcemoney.

In the words of Samuel P. Huntington, "These transnationalists have little need for national loyalty, view national boundaries as obstacles that thankfully are vanishing, and see national governments as residues from the past whose only useful function is to facilitate the elite's global operations."

To highlight the amount of fear that self-determination engenders in globalists, one only needs to look at the remarks given by newly minted U.S. President Barack Obama in his Nobel Peace Prize Lecture in 2009.

"Moreover, wars between nations have increasingly given way to wars within nations. The resurgence of ethnic or sectarian conflicts; the growth of secessionist movements, insurgencies, and failed states—all these things have increasingly trapped civilians in unending chaos."

With the inclusion of secession alongside violent revolutions and failed states such as Somalia, Obama echoed the globalist talking points on self-determination: it's dangerous, chaotic, and should be avoided at all costs. However, given the recent successes of Texit, Texans are of a different opinion.

TEXIT AND MAINSTREAM POLITICS

On the heels of the successful Brexit vote in June of 2016, Donald Trump, then the presumptive Republican nominee for president of the United States, visited Aberdeen, Scotland. During a press conference, a reporter asked Trump how he would react if Texans decided they wanted to Texit.

"Texas will never do that because Texas loves me."

While Trump, known for his off-the-cuff remarks, might not entirely believe that Texas' continued membership in the Union is entirely predicated on its love for him, the fact that the man who would go on to become the president of the United States was asked the question and commented on it was big news.

The larger story, however, was that a successful Brexit vote led to people in Texas calling for their own vote on Texit. News outlets throughout the United States echoed the party line. To them, a movement for Texit never existed until Brexit happened. At best, this was gross incompetence in reporting. At worst, it was malevolent by design. For each of the media outlets, it likely fell somewhere in between.

The fact is that, while Texas independence has been in the collective consciousness of Texans for decades, there have been some very recent examples of how the movement to make Texit a reality has entered into mainstream politics. All these happened prior to Brexit and prior to Trump's comment.

In 2009, then Governor Rick Perry stood in front of thousands of protesters at an anti-tax rally in Austin. As he was making a point about overreach by the federal government, someone in the crowd yelled, "Secede!" to an eruption of cheers and applause. When asked about the response by the media after the rally, Perry reiterated that he didn't support Texas leaving the Union, but reinforced his belief that it was a possibility if the federal government continued on its current path.

"I think there's a lot of different scenarios. Texas is a unique place. When we came into the Union in 1845, one of the issues was that we would be able to leave if we decided to do that. You know, my hope is that America and Washington in particular pays attention. We've got a great Union. There is absolutely no reason to dissolve it. But if Washington continues to thumb their nose at the American people, you know, who knows what may come out of that? But Texas is a very unique place and we're a pretty independent lot to boot."

This set off a firestorm in the media and among Perry's political opponents. Texas State Representative Jim Dunnam expressed his disdain for Perry's comments at a press conference.

"Talk of secession is an attack on our country. It can be nothing else. It is the ultimate anti-American statement."

He also didn't hold back when he speculated on Perry's motivations.

"We all knew he wanted to be president. I just didn't know it was president of the Republic of Texas."

Perry, a Republican, went on to win reelection to become the longest-serving governor in the history of Texas, and now is the Secretary of Energy in the Trump administration. Dunnam, a Democrat, lost his seat in the Texas House of Representatives the next year to his Republican challenger.

While expressing the possibility of Texit didn't hurt Perry politically, and there is no evidence to show that it directly helped him, there is some reason to believe that it energized his base, giving an indirect boost to his supporters at a time when he needed it. Much like Perry, there is no direct evidence that Dunnam was hurt by his opposition to Perry's comments or his hyperbolic attack on supporters of Texit. However, Dunnam lost his re-election bid by 1,648 votes. It is easy to imagine that, with Texit consistently polling solidly among independent and Republican voters, his remarks may have had enough of an impact to cost him the race.

This wouldn't be the last time public officials would be forced to comment on the issue. In 2011, the Obama administration launched an initiative called "We The People," an online system on whitehouse.gov that allowed citizens to create petitions. A petition receiving 25,000 signatures would elicit an official response from the White House.

In 2012, a petition was created calling for Texas to leave the Union. In short order, petitions were started for all 50 States and were getting signatures. The Texas petition soon received 126,000 signatures and five other States quickly reached the 25,000-vote threshold. Recognizing that the administration of a sitting U.S. president would be, under rules that he established, forced to issue a public statement on States leaving the Union, a media frenzy ensued.

Governors of States where the petition was gaining traction were asked about the issue, including Rick Perry. Perry echoed his comments from 2009, while other governors were caught flat-footed. Even presidential candidate Congressman Ron Paul was asked to chime in on the issue.

"It's very American to talk about secession—that's how we came into being," Representative Paul commented.

By January of 2013, White House Office of Public Engagement director Jon Carson issued the administration's official statement on the matter. In a 476-word response, Carson echoed the party line of the political establishment when he invoked the Supreme Court case of Texas v. White and declared that the Union was "perpetual." The statement added nothing new to the conversation and offered no arguments as to why any State should stay in the Union. Instead, it reestablished the tired, weak battle lines of the argument that has been the sole refrain from the pro-federal side for over a century.

As perpetual as the Union may seem to the Obama administration, it seems that Texans were of a different opinion. This fact wasn't missed by *New York Times* reporter Manny Fernandez in his story about the White House response.

"On the opening day of the Legislature here last Tuesday, supporters of the Texas Nationalist Movement—a group that wants Texas to sever its federal ties and become an independent nation—met with Republican leaders, including Lt. Gov. David Dewhurst. It was another sign that ideas once regarded as radical and even unpatriotic have found a measure of support, or at least sympathy, among some conservatives."

That support, still denied by the establishment, would become abundantly clear in 2015 as Texit grabbed international headlines from a source that few suspected—the State Republican Executive Committee (SREC). Following a statewide campaign by the TNM to force a non-binding vote on independence on the Republican Primary ballot, Tanya Robertson, SREC Committeewoman, submitted a resolution that would have done just that.

Although outwardly soft-spoken, Robertson had already gained a reputation as being uncompromising on liberty issues and is a fearless advocate for greater transparency within the Republican Party of Texas and a greater voice for the party in the creation and execution of public policy. Her uncompromising, principle-based approach has earned her the nickname "T-Rex" by her colleagues and foes alike.

Rather than being a shot in the dark on Texit, Robertson's resolution was more reflective of the sentiments of Texas Republicans than its critics would admit. Polling data has consistently shown that Republican voters in Texas support independence in large numbers. While the resolution didn't explicitly call for independence, it did express the sentiment that Texans, at the very least, should be able to publicly debate and vote on the issue.

Binding or not, Robertson's resolution ignited a media frenzy. In an interview with the *Houston Chronicle*, she was clear about her reason for submitting the proposal.

"There's been a big groundswell of Texans that are getting into the Texas independence issue. I believe conservatives in Texas should have a choice to voice their opinion."

Republican Chairman Tom Mechler was indignant, stating that he didn't believe that, "it would gain any traction." Much like he would do in 2016 at the Republican State Convention, Mechler pursued a strategy of "deny publicly, defy privately." However, on the first day of the SREC meeting, in full defiance of Mechler's prediction, the measure passed the Resolutions Committee, moving it to a full floor vote of the SREC and putting it one step closer to being on the ballot the following March.

The Resolutions Committee meeting wasn't free of drama, though. In an unprecedented act, the committee allowed public testimony only on this resolution. In addition, there were many proposed ballot resolutions on the table, including the hot button issues of abortion, transgender bathroom policy, school choice and gun-free zones, including a borderline exercise in narcissism by Governor Greg Abbott in the form of a resolution asking if voters supported his agenda. Due to the volume of proposals, the committee agreed to allow only the five that received the highest number of votes by the committee. Robertson's resolution was one of the five. Abbott's didn't make the cut.

Mechler was in a panic, as evidenced by his not-so-private dressing down of the committee chairman, Mark Ramsey, in the hallway. The next day would belong to Mechler, or so he thought. After a long night of backroom politicking, Mechler flipped enough votes to ensure the defeat of the measure by the full body of the SREC. But, as many often do, Mechler missed the point. The story, picked up and amplified by the media, was not solely that the measure was defeated. It was that more than one-third of the executive committee of the state's dominant political party voted in favor of Texans having a vote on independence.

This vote continues to resonate in Texas politics to this very day. During the subsequent campaign cycle, it became increasingly common for incumbents and challengers for seats in the Texas Legislature to be asked about Texit by the media.

One notable example came in the contest between State Representative John Frullo and former State Representative Jim Landtroop. Both were asked by KCBD News in Lubbock about whether they would support legislation for a referendum on Texas independence. Landtroop was emphatic in his support.

"I will fall on the sword for Texas' right to govern themselves. I am open to any measure or means necessary in order to do that."

Perhaps, with the consequences of Dunnam's full-throated denunciation of Rick Perry's remarks on the subject in his mind, Frullo chose to leave the door open.

"Secession is one of those things that we all like to talk about, we dream about we feel that we can do better individually as Texans and as well as a state if we didn't have Washington D.C. out there helping us. So that's the exciting part, if you look into the reality, it becomes a lot more complex."

Ever after the election, sitting elected officials were asked to sound off on the matter. After the post-Brexit Texit surge, Governor Abbott spoke with Fox News' host Sean Hannity on Hannity's radio show about the prospects of Texas independence where Hannity asked, "Do you think it ever gets to the point that the good people of Texas, and their values of freedom, separate themselves from the United States and go on their own?"

Abbott's answer came as a surprise. Rather than denouncing Texit or talking about the "greatness of the Union" like his predecessor, Abbott acknowledged the trend toward self-determination and self-government and the pain caused when it is ignored or denied.

"You brought up Brexit, this is something that's going on not just in the United States, but this is something that's going on across the entire globe and there's a reason for it. Sovereignty is a key component of a nation and we've seen the United States, we've seen Great Britain, we've seen countries in Europe sacrifice their sovereignty and we've seen the way their citizens have suffered because of it."

The flow of independence-related questions being put to elected officials didn't slow down after Brexit left the domestic news cycles. State representatives and senators have been fielding these questions ever since, not from the media, but from voters.

At a meeting of the Southeast Texas Tea Party in late 2016, State Representative Dade Phelan was forced to take a public position on the issue. When asked by a constituent if he supported Texas independence, he point blank expressed his opposition. However, in a follow-up question, he was asked, "If you represent us and enough of us want it, will you stand in the way?" Phelan, to his credit, stated that, as a representative of the district, if enough of his constituents wanted to vote on the issue, he would support legislation that would give them that opportunity.

Tanya Robertson's resolution and the subsequent convention fight came full circle to the Republican Party of Texas. In the spring of 2016, Mechler resigned as party chair. Although he didn't officially endorse a successor, Mechler made phone calls to the SREC members, advocating for Rick Figueroa. Figueroa is seen as a rising star among Republicans in Texas. He was a vocal advocate for Hispanic engagement in the Trump campaign machine, a demographic into which the state's Republicans are eager to tap. On the other side stood James Dickey, the chairman of the Republican Party of Travis County, in which the state's capitol is located, and a long-time political activist in Republican circles. While Dickey was supported by grassroots conservatives, Figueroa was lining up support from the political establishment.

During their final debate, held the night before the SREC vote, both candidates were asked about their position on the issue of Texas independence that had come up in Robertson's resolution and during the state convention. Figueroa gave an emphatic denunciation. Dickey answered that, as the chair, it wouldn't be his place to make that decision and that he would leave it up to the will of the body. The next day, James Dickey was elected as the new chair of the Republican Party of Texas.

Texit had arrived.

2 | UNDERSTANDING THE AMERICAN UNION

> 66 ...a long habit of not thinking a thing wrong, gives it a superficial appearance of being right, and raises at first a formidable outcry in defense of custom. But the tumult soon subsides. Time makes more converts than reason. 99
>
> *Thomas Paine*

I'm going to describe a political entity to you but I'm not going to tell you its name. Let's see if you can get it. This is a union of many States who enjoy free trade and travel among one another. They send elected representatives to a specific city who make laws, rules and regulations for all of them. They have a judiciary system and diplomatic relations with other countries around the world. They have a common passport, a common defense, and a common currency.

Were you able to guess it? If you said the European Union, you were correct. If you said the United States of America, you were also correct. This was an important exercise in equivalencies. While Brexit bolstered the hopes of many who support Texit, the skeptics were quick to make the assertion that the two were too different to compare. The reason for their emphatic declaration was that the European Union and the United States of America were vastly different institutions. Fundamentally, they are wrong.

To understand how a modern-day Texit can happen, it is necessary to understand the Union to which Texas belongs. This requires addressing some commonly held misconceptions about its nature, its purpose, its founding, and its current status.

In the Biblical book of Genesis, we are told the story of the Tower of Babel. From the moment small children learn the story in Sunday school, they are taught that it is a cautionary tale about the folly of humans aspiring to godhood. However, as adults, and in the context of modern political understanding, I would submit that it teaches us an additional lesson.

In the story, when God saw that the people were constructing a tower to Heaven, he cursed them in such a way as to prevent their cooperation: he "confused their tongues," causing them all to speak different languages. Suddenly struck with an inability to communicate, the people gave up on construction of the tower and scattered among the Earth.

When people don't speak the same language, it is impossible to have meaningful discussion and dialog. We see that in today's political discourse. Although here we speak English, we cannot agree on common definitions. Liberal, a word once reserved for those who wanted to liberate power from the central authority and return it to the people, has come to mean something completely different in today's context. Conservative has become such a watered-down term that even politicians with horrendous voting records on fiscal and social conservatism can claim the mantle of "true conservative" and do so with a straight face. Marxist and Maoist political philosophy has been repackaged and rebranded as Progressivism. Yet, if you were to ask 100 different people on the street to define any of these words, you would get a broad set of answers. Expand your question to 300 million people spread across 50 different States, and the variation in answers would make you wonder if you were even speaking the same language.

Every day, people say the words "United States" and "America" and never give a second thought to what those words actually mean. If you ask the average person on the street, they have to pause to give it thought as though they were solving a math problem. Yet people still pledge allegiance to its flag, sing its anthem, and declare their undying loyalty and support for it.

The reason that so many have a challenge with defining these words is that their meaning is not as simple as it may seem on the surface. Two hundred thirty years ago, the "united States of America" had a very clear meaning. Its creators understood their creation and all of its legal and philosophical implications. In the intervening years, their clarity has given way to confusion and their concrete vision has been replaced by a superficial affinity to the trappings of that vision. The principles they sought to embody in their "united States of America" have been largely abandoned for a popular love of the pomp and circumstance that alleges to celebrate them.

Statements such as these qualify as a modern-day heresy and invite the charge of being un-American. Yet those who are quickest to level the charge are generally the same who can't tell you what it means to be an American. Do they mean American in the sense that one lives in America or is a citizen of the United States? Do they mean American in the sense that one adheres to American principles? Do they mean American in the sense that one pledges unquestioning obedience to the federal government?

They will likely be ignorant of the fact that those who founded the "united States" echoed the same concerns as they feared for what would become of their creation in future generations. In fact, it was George Washington who warned us all to, "Guard against the impostures of pretended patriotism."

Imagine the surprise that those who founded the "united States" would have if they saw that many conceptualize the Union as a solitary, monolithic nation-state with its 50 States essentially considered provinces or administrative subdivisions. In the language of their day and in their understanding when they created the Union, the States were the equivalent of modern-day nation-states with all the sovereignty and rights that implies.

Therein lies the problem. The difficulty that many have with conceptualizing Texit is that they have a hard time conceptualizing the Union of which Texas is a member. Many are under the delusion that the United States is a nation-state unto itself and not a collection of nation-states. Even the most vociferous advocates of the single-state ideology struggle to explain away the plain evidence to the contrary. Why is it called the United States of America as opposed to the United State of America or simply America? Why are there 50 stars on the flag as opposed to 1? Why is there still a United States Senate comprised of members who represent their respective States? Why is there an electoral college? Why are States still required to engage one another in matters outside the purview of the federal government through interstate compacts? Why does each State still have its own constitution with its own laws and its own three branches of government?

If the United States of America is a nation-state, it has a national government and the States possess no sovereignty. They are merely administrative subdivisions of national government, operating at the pleasure of the federal government with no true identity or voice of their own.

This distinction is clearly made in Black's Law Dictionary.

"A national government is a government of the people of a single state or nation, united as a community by what is termed the 'social compact,' and possessing complete and perfect supremacy over persons and things, so far as they can be made the lawful objects of civil government. A federal government is distinguished from a national government by its being the government of a community of independent and sovereign states, united by compact."

If the United States of America is a federative republic, then the States created both the Union and the federal government, and each State still possesses its identity, sovereignty, and rights. The two conditions are mutually exclusive. They both cannot be true.

In 2013, then President Barack Obama gave a speech at the dedication of the George W. Bush Presidential Library. His remarks were fairly unremarkable except for one word—"these." As is tradition, he ended his speech with the words "God bless these United States."

While the slight difference between "the" and "these" went unnoticed by most, the word change and its significance didn't escape the eye of Andrew Burt at *The Atlantic*.

"The significance lies in the difference between "the" and "these," between referring to the United States as a singular entity or in the plural—a difference with a long history, and one with huge implications. The language we use to talk about ourselves as a country, after all, provides one of the clearest windows into how we see ourselves as a nation and as a people. It was the Articles of Confederation that first gave rise to the United States, but it is the article that precedes "United States" that tells our story—and ultimately, that provides insight into Obama's presidency and the increasing polarization of Americans today."

No matter how far removed the policies of the Obama administration may have been from the original vision of the Founding Fathers, in this instance he was on the money. The Union was referred to in its plural form until it was drummed out of popular usage during the Second World War. There it lay dormant until the 1980s where it began to re-enter usage under the Reagan presidency.

Whether the singular or plural is used in referring to the Union seems like a trivial matter. Yet it is key to understanding the Union. In fact, it was Reagan who, philosophically and publicly, broke with the post-Civil War trend of placing the United States federal government at the apex of power. Breaking with the historical revisionists who believed the federal government magically created the States, Reagan declared in his first inaugural address, "All of us need to be reminded that the Federal Government did not create the States; the States created the Federal Government."

Reagan's distinction is as important as Obama's, since both echo the truth about the creation of the Union. From its inception in the Declaration of Independence, the Union was one of independent and sovereign States. Jefferson was clear in drafting the declaration when he wrote:

"That these united Colonies are, and of Right ought to be Free and Independent States, that they are Absolved from all Allegiance to the British Crown, and that all political connection between them and the State of Great Britain, is and ought to be totally dissolved; and that as Free and Independent States, they have full Power to levy War, conclude Peace, contract Alliances, establish Commerce, and to do all other Acts and Things which Independent States may of right do."

This was acknowledged and understood by Great Britain in the Treaty of Paris that ended the American Revolution and validated the independence of the 13 individual colonies.

"His Brittanic Majesty acknowledges the said United States, viz., New Hampshire, Massachusetts Bay, Rhode Island and Providence Plantations, Connecticut, New York, New Jersey, Pennsylvania, Delaware, Maryland, Virginia, North Carolina, South Carolina and Georgia, to be free sovereign and Independent States; that he treats with them as such, and for himself his Heirs & Successors, relinquishes all claims to the Government, Propriety, and Territorial Rights of the same and every Part thereof."

These States went on to create a framework under which they would collectively operate, called the Articles of Confederation. In the Articles, the States instituted a process of cooperation in affairs that affected them all, stating, "The said States hereby severally enter into a firm league of friendship with each other, for their common defense, the security of their liberties, and their mutual and general welfare, binding themselves to assist each other, against all force offered to, or attacks made upon them, or any of them, on account of religion, sovereignty, trade, or any other pretense whatever."

When the idealism of the Articles of Confederation met the reality of administering a union of 13 newly independent States, it proved ineffective. Its many shortcomings led directly to the movement to replace the entire document. Ostensibly convening to discuss how to amend the Articles of Confederation, delegates actually exceeded their mandate from their respective States and drafted an entirely new document.

The Constitution of the United States was drafted as a remedial document to directly address the shortcomings of the Articles of Confederation. That included the ratification clause as well. Where the Articles of Confederation required the ratification of all 13 States, the Constitution only required ratification by 9 of the 13 to enter into effect. Had only 9 of the States ratified the document, only those 9 States would have lived under the Constitution and the remaining 4 would have remained under an Articles of Confederation that no longer had enough members to operate.

While the Constitution was more effective than the Articles of Confederation at managing a union, the fundamental construction was the same. It was a union of sovereign, independent States that created a framework to collectively address common issues.

If this sounds remotely familiar, it should. This concept is at the heart of every multilateral treaty ever executed. The North Atlantic Treaty Organization (NATO) was created as a military alliance to provide a common defense for its members, which has now expanded to 29 nations. The United Nations was created as a multinational body to establish a framework for international cooperation on the issues of conflict resolution, human rights, and general welfare. Both are multilateral treaties of which the United States is a signatory. Although there is no definitive number of multilateral treaties of which the United States is a part, some estimates place the number between 200 and 500. Each is an agreement between nation-states that establishes an operating framework for one or more aspects of their relationship.

In much the same way, the American States created the Union and drafted a constitution as the governing rules for that Union. In that constitution, they created a federal government to administer very specific functions in the document and gave it 30 specific powers with which to accomplish the task. Taken directly from the document, the federal government was given the authority to do the following:

- To lay and collect Taxes, Duties, Imposts and Excises, to pay the Debts and provide for the common Defence and general Welfare of the United States; but all Duties, Imposts and Excises shall be uniform throughout the United States;

- To borrow Money on the credit of the United States;

- To regulate Commerce with foreign Nations, and among the several States, and with the Indian Tribes;

- To establish an uniform Rule of Naturalization, and uniform Laws on the subject of Bankruptcies throughout the United States;

- To coin Money, regulate the Value thereof, and of foreign Coin, and fix the Standard of Weights and Measures;

- To provide for the Punishment of counterfeiting the Securities and current Coin of the United States;

- To establish Post Offices and post Roads;

- To promote the Progress of Science and useful Arts, by securing for limited Times to Authors and Inventors the exclusive Right to their respective Writings and Discoveries;

- To constitute Tribunals inferior to the supreme Court;

- To define and punish Piracies and Felonies committed on the high Seas, and Offences against the Law of Nations;

- To declare War, grant Letters of Marque and Reprisal, and make Rules concerning Captures on Land and Water;

- To raise and support Armies, but no Appropriation of Money to that Use shall be for a longer Term than two Years;

- To provide and maintain a Navy;

- To make Rules for the Government and Regulation of the land and naval Forces;

- To provide for calling forth the Militia to execute the Laws of the Union, suppress Insurrections and repel Invasions;

- To provide for organizing, arming, and disciplining, the Militia, and for governing such Part of them as may be employed in the Service of the United States, reserving to the States respectively, the Appointment of the Officers, and the Authority of training the Militia according to the discipline prescribed by Congress;

- To exercise exclusive Legislation in all Cases whatsoever, over such District (not exceeding ten Miles square) as may, by Cession of particular States, and the Acceptance of Congress, become the Seat of the Government of the United States, and to exercise like Authority over all Places purchased by the Consent of the Legislature of the State in which the Same shall be, for the Erection of Forts, Magazines, Arsenals, dock-Yards, and other needful Buildings; And

- To make all Laws which shall be necessary and proper for carrying into Execution the foregoing Powers, and all other Powers vested by this Constitution in the Government of the United States, or in any Department or Officer thereof.

- No State shall, without the Consent of the Congress, lay any Imposts or Duties on Imports or Exports, except what may be absolutely necessary for executing its inspection Laws: and the net Produce of all Duties and Imposts, laid by any State on Imports or Exports, shall be for the Use of the Treasury of the United States; and all such Laws shall be subject to the Revision and Control of the Congress.

- The Congress may determine the Time of chusing the Electors, and the Day on which they shall give their Votes; which Day shall be the same throughout the United States.

- In Case of the Removal of the President from Office, or of his Death, Resignation, or Inability to discharge the Powers and Duties of the said Office, the Same shall devolve on the Vice President, and the Congress may by Law provide for the Case of Removal, Death, Resignation or Inability, both of the President and Vice President, declaring what Officer shall then act as President, and such Officer shall act accordingly, until the Disability be removed, or a President shall be elected.

- The judicial Power of the United States, shall be vested in one supreme Court, and in such inferior Courts as the Congress may from time to time ordain and establish.

- The Trial of all Crimes, except in Cases of Impeachment, shall be by Jury; and such Trial shall be held in the State where the said Crimes shall have been committed; but when not committed within any State, the Trial shall be at such Place or Places as the Congress may by Law have directed.

- The Congress shall have Power to declare the Punishment of Treason, but no Attainder of Treason shall work Corruption of Blood, or Forfeiture except during the Life of the Person attainted.

- Full Faith and Credit shall be given in each State to the public Acts, Records, and judicial Proceedings of every other State. And the Congress may by general Laws prescribe the Manner in which such Acts, Records, and Proceedings shall be proved, and the Effect thereof.

- New States may be admitted by the Congress into this Union;

- The Congress shall have Power to dispose of and make all needful Rules and Regulations respecting the Territory or other Property belonging to the United States; and nothing in this Constitution shall be so construed as to Prejudice any Claims of the United States, or of any particular State.

- The Congress, whenever two thirds of both Houses shall deem it necessary, shall propose Amendments to this Constitution, or, on the Application of the Legislatures of two thirds of the several States, shall call a Convention for proposing Amendments, which, in either Case, shall be valid to all Intents and Purposes, as Part of this Constitution, when ratified by the Legislatures of three fourths of the several States, or by Conventions in three fourths thereof, as the one or the other Mode of Ratification may be proposed by the Congress

- The House of Representatives shall chuse their Speaker and other Officers; and shall have the sole Power of Impeachment...

- The Senate shall have the sole Power to try all Impeachments. When sitting for that Purpose, they shall be on Oath or Affirmation. When the President of the United States is tried, the Chief Justice shall preside: And no Person shall be convicted without the Concurrence of two thirds of the Members present.

- The Times, Places and Manner of holding Elections for Senators and Representatives, shall be prescribed in each State by the Legislature thereof; but the Congress may at any time by Law make or alter such Regulations, except as to the Places of chusing Senators.

Because of these specific grants of authority and to avoid overlap, the Constitution lists very specific actions from which the States are prohibited from engaging. These are specifically listed in Article 1, Section 10.

- No State shall enter into any Treaty, Alliance, or Confederation; grant Letters of Marque and Reprisal; coin Money; emit Bills of Credit; make any Thing but gold and silver Coin a Tender in Payment of Debts; pass any Bill of Attainder, ex post facto Law, or Law impairing the Obligation of Contracts, or grant any Title of Nobility.

- No State shall, without the Consent of the Congress, lay any Imposts or Duties on Imports or Exports, except what may be

absolutely necessary for executing its inspection Laws: and
the net Produce of all Duties and Imposts, laid by any State
on Imports or Exports, shall be for the Use of the Treasury of
the United States; and all such Laws shall be subject to the
Revision and Control of the Congress.

- No State shall, without the Consent of Congress, lay any duty
  of Tonnage, keep Troops, or Ships of War in time of Peace,
  enter into any Agreement or Compact with another State,
  or with a foreign Power, or engage in War, unless actually
  invaded, or in such imminent Danger as will not admit of
  delay."

With the final caveat being that all States must have a "republican
form of government," all other powers were reserved to the States. To
ensure that it would never be forgotten, it was enshrined in the Tenth
Amendment to the Constitution and cemented as a part of the Bill of
Rights.

"The powers not delegated to the United States by the Constitution,
nor prohibited by it to the States, are reserved to the States respectively,
or to the people."

In arguing for the inclusion of language to the Constitution that
would explicitly reserve sovereignty to the States, Fisher Ames, in the
ratification convention of Massachusetts said:

"A consolidation of the States would subvert the new Constitution,
and against which this article is our best security. Too much provision
cannot be made against consolidation. The State Governments represent the wishes and feelings, and local interests of the people. They are
the safeguard and ornament of the Constitution; they will protract the
period of our liberties; they will afford a shelter against the abuse of
power, and will be the natural avengers of our violated rights."

Neither the current operations of the federal government, past legal decisions of the Supreme Court, historical revisionism, nor commonly held fallacies change the fundamental structure of the Union as a voluntary political and economic union comprised of independent, sovereign States, each containing a separate and distinct people.

Even Alexander Hamilton, who dreamed of a single nation with the States merely functioning as corporations, conceded the distinct and sovereign existence of the States in Federalist #32.

"An entire consolidation of the States into one complete national sovereignty would imply an entire subordination of the parts; and whatever powers might remain in them, would be altogether dependent on the general will. But the plan of the convention aims only at a partial union or consolidation, the State governments would clearly retain all rights of sovereignty which they before had, and which were not, by that act, exclusively delegated to the United States."

We need only look to the words of James Madison, the "Father of the Constitution" and the fourth president of the United States, for confirmation.

"Each State, in ratifying the Constitution, is considered as a sovereign body, independent of all others, and only to be bound by its own voluntary act. In this relation, then, the new Constitution will, if established, be a federal, and not a national constitution."

He and the other Founding Fathers understood what being a "State" meant in the context of the United States. While the language has evolved, the meaning of the term in their day is still important. States of the United States are called States for a reason. They were not and still are not called provinces, territories, divisions, or regions. In fact, referring back to the Declaration of Independence, we see Jefferson refer to Great Britain as the "State of Great Britain" making it clear that individual States of the Union are each equal in all respects to Great Britain.

Texans who colonized the then Mexican state carried this concept with them. Stephen F. Austin, writing in 1836, elaborated on this concept of statehood when citing the sources of the conflict between Texas and the Mexican government.

"When the federal system and constitution were adopted in 1824, and the former provinces became states, Texas, by her representative in the constituent congress, exercised the right which was claimed and exercised by all the provinces, of retaining within her own control, the rights and powers which appertained to her as one of the unities or distinct societies, which confederated together to form the federal republic of Mexico. But not possessing at that time sufficient population to become a state by herself, she was with her own consent, united provisionally with Coahuila, a neighbouring province or society, to form the state of COAHUILA AND TEXAS, "until Texas possessed the necessary elements to form a separate state of herself."

"I quote the words of the constitutional or organic act passed by the constituent congress of Mexico, on the 7th of May, 1824, which establishes the state of Coahuila and Texas. This law, and the principles on which the Mexican federal compact was formed, gave Texas a specific political existence, and vested in her inhabitants the special and well-defined rights of self-government as a state of the Mexican confederation, so soon as she "possessed the necessary elements." Texas consented to the provisional union with Coahuila on the faith of this guarantee. It was therefore a solemn compact, which neither the state of Coahuila and Texas, nor the general government of Mexico, can change without the consent of the people of Texas."

The Mexican government's failure to abide by its agreement with the people of Texas and to recognize their "specific political existence" as a State led directly to the Texas Revolution and Texas declaring its independence. It is this meaning of "State" that Texans understood when they made a conscious choice to join the Union. Texans understood that their State would continue to be a sovereign political entity when it entered into the Union, just like all of the other States who were currently in the union. This was a guarantee given in the Joint Resolution of Annexation when the United States Congress declared that Texas was "admitted into the Union, by virtue of this act, on an equal footing with the existing states."

However, the post-war Texas Constitution shatters this idea in its very first lines. Article 1, Section 1 of the Texas Constitution of 1876 declares:

"Texas is a free and independent State, subject only to the Constitution of the United States, and the maintenance of our free institutions and the perpetuity of the Union depend upon the preservation of the right of local self-government, unimpaired to all the States."

Texas is a free, independent, and sovereign State in a political and economic union with 49 other free, independent, and sovereign States. Collectively, these States work together to common ends and to solve common challenges. They operate under a framework that is codified in the Constitution of the United States. This framework created a federal government whose job it is to administer the Union in very specific ways. Anything beyond that, the States are, in every respect, like any other sovereign nation-state anywhere else in the world.

We are not, nor were we ever intended to be, one nation. Madison clearly articulated this fact and the rationale behind labeling it as fallacy.

"First, in order to ascertain the real character of the government, it may be considered in relation to the foundation on which it is to be established; to the sources from which its ordinary powers are to be drawn; to the operation of those powers; to the extent of them; and to the authority by which future changes in the government are to be introduced... On examining the first relation, it appears, on one hand, that the Constitution is to be founded on the assent and ratification of the people of America, given by deputies elected for the special purpose; but, on the other, that this assent and ratification is to be given by the people, not as individuals composing one entire nation, but as composing the distinct and independent States to which they respectively belong. It is to be the assent and ratification of the several States, derived from the supreme authority in each State, the authority of the people themselves. The act, therefore, establishing the Constitution, will not be a national, but a federal act. That it will be a federal and not a national act, as these terms are understood by the objectors; the act of the people, as forming so many independent States, not as forming one aggregate nation, is obvious from this single consideration, that it is to result neither from the decision of a majority of the people of the Union, nor from that of a majority of the States. It must result from the unanimous assent of the several States that are parties to it, differing no otherwise from their ordinary assent than in its being expressed, not by the legislative authority, but by that of the people themselves. Were the people regarded in this transaction as forming one nation, the will of the majority of the whole people of the United States would bind the minority, in the same manner as the majority in each State must bind the minority; and the will of the majority must be determined either by a comparison of the individual votes, or by considering the will of the majority of the States as evidence of the will of a majority of the people of the United States. Neither of these rules have been adopted. Each State, in ratifying the Constitution, is considered as a sovereign body, independent of all others, and only to be bound by its own voluntary act. In this relation, then, the new Constitution will, if established, be a federal, and not a national constitution."

The idea of an American nation was a fringe idea at best until the Civil War. After the Civil War, it became trendy to promote the idea of an American nation in an attempt to heal the wounds caused by the war and to retroactively justify the prosecution of the war. However, no single person contributed more to this idea than a late-19th century Christian Socialist who had been removed from the pulpit as a Baptist minister for delivering sermons on topics such as "Jesus the Socialist." That failed minister was Francis Bellamy.

Bellamy was not nearly as well known at the time as his cousin, Edward Bellamy, who had the second bestselling book of the 1800s, *Looking Backward*. The book envisions a future United States where everyone has equal incomes and, at the age of 21, men are conscripted into an "industrial army," working in jobs assigned to them by the federal government. Bellamy's book was an inspiration to many who, in the spirit of his work, began to found "Nationalist Clubs" promoting Bellamy's ideals and advocating for a government takeover of the economy. Francis would found a Nationalist Club of his own in Boston.

Shortly after the founding of the Nationalist Club in Boston, Francis looked for a way to promote Edward's vision to the youth of the day. Francis Bellamy penned these words for *Youth's Companion*, a popular children's magazine:

"I pledge allegiance to my Flag and the Republic for which it stands, one nation, indivisible, with liberty and justice for all."

With the help of the magazine and the National Education Association, Bellamy was able to promote the pledge to public schools throughout the United States with these explicit instructions as to how it was to be given.

"At a signal from the Principal the pupils, in ordered ranks, hands to the side, face the Flag. Another signal is given; every pupil gives the Flag the military salute—right hand lifted, palm downward, to a line with the forehead and close to it... At the words, 'to my Flag,' the right hand is extended gracefully, palm upward, towards the Flag, and remains in this gesture till the end of the affirmation; whereupon all hands immediately drop to the side."

Bellamy's pledge became wildly popular. In 1923, words were added to specify the flag of the United States. However, in the 1930s, another change was instituted as some began to notice similarities between Bellamy's salute and another salute that had become quite popular in Europe—the fascist salute.

In fact, the pledge, the ceremony, and the ideals Bellamy sought to promote with it are well known to us today as fascism. The nationalization of industries and the incorporation of workers into a massive labor army were major programs of the German National Socialists, Mussolini's Italian Fascists, and Roosevelt's New Deal. Without a doubt, Bellamy's vision of a radical nationalist state with a socialist economic system has more in common with Hitler and FDR than with Washington, Madison, and Jefferson's vision of the United States. Yet his greatest tool for promotion of this ideology is recited daily by schoolchildren throughout the United States to this very day.

As a tool of indoctrination into the cult of the "one nation" doctrine, it has been extremely effective. It is not uncommon to hear a well-meaning opponent of Texit recite the Pledge of Allegiance as though it were law followed by an imaginary "mic drop" like they uttered something truly profound. But it is not law nor does it inform the actual conversation about the existence of an American nation one iota.

The fact is that there is no "American people." There are people who live on the North American continent, but that also includes Canadians and Mexicans. There are people who live within the political union called the United States of America. Perhaps those are the Americans. But to say that America is one nation, a single, homogenous and well-defined people, is a massive stretch. If we are "one people," then it seems unusual that we would all readily identify ourselves as something other than simply American.

While "American" is a handy term, much like "European" or "Asian," it ignores the fact that those who most would call "American" more regularly identify themselves and others as something other than "American." People in Texas clearly identify themselves as Texans. People in South Louisiana are quick to identify themselves as Cajuns. People across the southern States clearly identify themselves as Southerners, just as folks in the Midwest identify themselves as Midwesterners. Californians are some of the quickest to let a person know that they identify with their home State.

The divisions are more pronounced than it would initially seem, and they are not isolated to geography. In the wake of the 2016 presidential election, *Bloomberg Businessweek* published a series of articles called "One Nation Divisible." In an attempt to see just how divided Americans are, they separated the most common terms for self-identification and then extrapolated the total number of possible combinations. Their results were insightful.

"We categorized Americans using these five divisions: red state or blue state, old or young, rich or not-rich, white or minority, male or female. Arrange those groups in every possible combination—old men, red-state young women, old rich minority men, blue-state young rich white women, etc.—and you wind up with 242 different Americas."

More and more, these differences are becoming harder to ignore. Whether it's in politics, policy, or principles, the idea that America is one people and one nation is an increasingly harder sell. When Travis wrote his famous letter from the Alamo, he called for aid "in the name of Liberty, of patriotism, & everything dear to the American character…" If he wrote that same letter today, it's not entirely clear what he would get when appealing to the American character.

Herein lies the fundamental challenge with understanding the

American union, especially in the context of Texit. The lack of clarity in language creates a moving target, stifles legitimate debate on the relationship of the States within the Union, and serves to conceal the damage done by the federal government to the rights of the States and the people.

When one talks about America, the question arises as to which America we're talking about. There is America the landmass with its "amber waves of grain." There are the ideals of freedom, liberty, and representative government that we typically classify as "American." Then there is the "United States of America," the political and economic union embodied in the federal government.

Although these are separate and distinct viewpoints, the tendency is to treat them all as one and the same. The effect is chilling. If you criticize the political and economic union or the actions of the federal government, you are branded as un-American, as though by daring to question the effectiveness or actions of the government you are somehow the moral equivalent of the Islamic State trying to destroy the ideals upon which the Union was originally founded. Even when the actions of the Union are contrary and diametrically opposed to the generally recognized American principles upon which the Union was founded, criticism to the point of advocating exiting the Union invites the slur and the hurling of the pejorative—"secessionist."

Prior to the widespread use of the term "Texit," anything related to Texas independence was classified using the word "secession." However, Texit and secession are not entirely synonymous and it is an important distinction. It depends on how you define the actual relationship between the States of the United States.

If you believe that the United States of America is a monolithic nation-state and the States are merely administrative subdivisions of the federal government, then secession is your term. However, if you

83

believe the United States of America is a federated republic of sovereign, independent States who delegated specific, limited powers to a federal government, and any other powers reside with the States, then Texit is your term.

In her September 2000 paper "Who, Why and How: Assessing the Legitimacy of Secession," Dr. Josette Baer, professor of political theory at the University of Zurich in Switzerland, highlighted the nuanced difference and its impact on any legitimate discussion on the issue.

"For the sake of clearly limited terms, let me shortly explain, why I do not consider 'secession' as appropriate a term when dealing with supranational political buildings like the European Union or the Commonwealth of Independent States. One could argue that the decision to leave such a structure represents indeed a secession since it zeals at the regaining of the amount of sovereignty once ceded by virtue of the membership treaties agreed upon. However, the crucial thing in this matter has to do with the nature of these structures and the amount of sovereignty: the amount of sovereignty ceded to a supranational building differs quantitatively from sovereignty established by state-building. It also differs qualitatively, because the decision to enter the union has been met by sovereign states which expressed their consent by committing themselves to agreements whose details and conditions they were able to negotiate... For the leave of a supranational building I therefore would suggest to speak of cancellation of membership rather than of secession."

This distinction makes Texit more like the U.K.'s exit from the European Union. In the 21st century, and especially in its application to what's taking place in Texas, this is an important distinction to make. If Texit is secession from a monolithic nation-state, then it renders the Founding Fathers' original intent for the Union irrelevant and cedes any sovereignty retained by Texas upon its original entry into the Union completely and totally to the federal government. If Texit is a withdrawal of membership from a political and economic union that has overstepped its bounds, we are able to claim the original sovereignty of the State, and set the stage for the battle over Texit as an acceptance or rejection by the federal government of the original intent of the Union.

In short, someone's attitude toward Texit is often directly tied to his or her understanding of the American Union. If one understands that it is based on a fundamental ignorance of the original purpose of the Union, then they will likely oppose any discussion of Texit at a visceral level. If, however, one understands the true origins and purpose of the United States, then they can clearly see how vastly today's American Union has strayed from its original course and then Texit becomes a discussion that must be had, not only for Texas, but for every State in the United States.

3 | CAUSES WHICH IMPEL THEM

66When the Federal Republican Constitution of their country, which they have sworn to support, no longer has a substantial existence, and the whole nature of their government has been forcibly changed, without their consent, from a restricted federative republic, composed of sovereign states, to a consolidated central military despotism...99

Texas Declaration of Independence, March 2, 1836

I have been asked by the media many times to explain why support for Texit has grown into a major political issue. I have often thought about how ludicrous it is for them to ask that question and expect a one- or two-sentence answer. Honestly, it would take multiple books to detail all the grievances Texans have with the federal system and to point out all the ways that it has and continues to fail. By the time it was written, it would be out of date and in need of expansion. However, it can be boiled down to its essence.

"The people of Texas are tired of living under 180,000 pages of federal laws, administered by 440 separate federal agencies and 2.5 million unelected bureaucrats. The people of Texas are sick of having their lives dictated by politicians they didn't elect forcing policies on them that they don't want."

At a very basic level, harkening back to their history, Texans don't like to be told what to do, when to do it, or how to do it. They want to govern themselves. They also acknowledge that there is a very limited role for government. However, Texans bristle at both the perception and reality of what governance has become. Perception is as strong, if not stronger, than reality, and the reality is worse than most perceive.

Author and Texas-based entrepreneur David Thomas Roberts expressed the sentiments of the vast majority of Texans when he wrote:

"Our income and our labors are taxed and redistributed to those who won't work, to inefficient and corrupt governmental agencies, to programs that might violate our faith and to morally despicable foreign governments—of which many hate us despite the money we give them."

"This marriage has run its course," agrees author Paul Vandevelder in a 2012 op-ed for the *Los Angeles Times*. "Too many niggling little things built up over time, driving us all crazy. So let's just stop. It's time to divvy up the china and draft a property settlement."

The systemic problems with the Union stand in stark contrast to the success story of Texas. Sure, Texas has its issues, but increasingly our issues are being seen as a function of our membership in the Union and our success and prosperity in spite of it. This causes Texans to look at the federal government with deep-seated distrust and ever-growing contempt.

This attitude was perfectly captured by Chuck Pool, a columnist with the *Arlington Voice*. "This 'nation,' as some would call it, is not only a highly functional, world-class economy, engaging in robust commerce with other nations and neighboring states, it actually has a budget, a balanced one at that," he wrote. "...why should the Great Republic of Texas continue to be at the losing end of the welfare wormhole that wends its way to New York and other so-called blue states by way of the Washington vortex?"

The perception is that the federal government is inefficient, ineffective, incompetent, and incapable of understanding the needs and desires of the people under its umbrella. The reality is far worse.

With all of its faults, the federal government continues to assume more control over every facet of daily life and assert more authority over the lives of hard-working individuals. In its desire to control everything and everyone, it extracts more taxes to fund its efforts, rendering even the most productive, hard-working among us as mere vassals in a massive feudal state. All of this is to buy the loyalty of the thumb-suckers, whiners, and social experimenters who refuse to produce, refuse to compete, and reject any notion of personal accountability.

Crushed under the weight of the bureaucracy necessary to administer their superstate, individual initiative is stifled, dissention is suppressed, and any hope of internal reform that strips power from the federal machine withers and dies.

To ensure total control, the federal government has converted the checks and balances of the three-branch government into agencies of manufactured dissent to give the semblance of choice but, in practice, acts as a rubber-stamp for policies that centralize more control in the halls of Washington, D.C.

In the name of national security and in violation of its own laws and constitutionally guaranteed protections against illegal search and seizure, the federal government has admittedly intercepted every electronic communication made by every citizen. Yet the borders are still porous, allowing virtually unrestricted migration, leaving citizens as the ones required to bear the full weight of the national security state.

Christian principles, once the bedrock of our society, are denigrated as anachronistic, except for "love thy neighbor," but only when it applies to someone who is part of the latest pet cause as dictated by the Hollywood elites. But it's never if your neighbor is an unborn child, a member of the opposite political party, or a follower of the person who uttered those words in the first place. Those who, following the example of the Founders of the American Union, invoke God in the public sphere are mercilessly mocked, unless their god is Allah, Satan, a head of cabbage, or themselves.

This system has relegated State elected officials, the first line of defense against federal overreach in a federative republic, to the role of caretakers and administrators of federal policy. It has bribed them into compliance with the hope that one day, they too might feed at the federal money trough in Washington as a congressman, senator, or even president.

Given the nearly unrestricted power of lawmaking and taxation, they ensure that actual dissent is nearly nonexistent. Every citizen has become a federal lawbreaker and we are suffocated under a tax code that few have actually read and no one fully understands. Like the Sword of Damocles, federal retribution hangs over the heads of everyone, waiting to impale anyone who steps out of line.

This is the true "thought crime" of Texit supporters. It is perfectly fashionable in conservative circles to question the actions of the federal government when the Democrats are in charge. It's even more fashionable for liberals to "resist" when Republicans hold the reins. Bookstores are filled with anti-government screeds from every mid-level politician looking for a promotion. The airwaves are filled with pundits who slam the D.C. machine for every action or inaction. However, questioning whether Texas should be a part of this machine is, somehow, "a bridge too far."

The bridge is getting closer. By heaping piles of injustice, indignity, and indecision on Texans, the federal government, and the people of the United States themselves, are making the case for Texit daily. Ian Baldwin and Frank Bryan, writing for the *Washington Post*, summed it up.

"The winds of secession are blowing... Over the past 50 years, the U.S. government has grown too big, too corrupt and too aggressive toward the world, toward its own citizens and toward local democratic institutions. It has abandoned the democratic vision of its founders and eroded Americans' fundamental freedoms..."

THE FEDERAL SUPERSTATE

In the midst of the fight over the Affordable Care Act, known colloquially as Obamacare, Judge Andrew Napolitano interviewed South Carolina Congressman Jim Clyburn, the number three ranking Democrat in Congress, on the Fox News Channel. Napolitano posed a question to the congressman, "Where in the Constitution is the federal government authorized to manage healthcare?"

His response? "Most of what we do down here isn't authorized by the Constitution."

"Congressman, don't you remember that you took an oath to uphold the Constitution?" Napolitano asked.

"Yes, but you tell me where in the Constitution it is prohibited for the federal government to manage healthcare."

Sadly enough, exchanges such as this are far too common. When push comes to shove, even the staunchest conservatives in the federal government fall back on their belief in a virtually unlimited power center in Washington. When power is concentrated and expanded in this manner, it requires a massive bureaucracy to oversee its operations.

To classify the federal bureaucracy as massive is, in itself, a massive understatement. As with many things related to the federal government, current and accurate numbers are hard to come by. Officially, the federal government employs approximately 2.6 million workers, in addition to a large number of government contractors. This number is actually a fraction of the actual size of bureaucracy. An internal government report in 2005 noted that all segments of the federal government actually employed approximately 14.6 million people. That included 1.9 million civil servants, 770,000 postal workers, 1.44 million uniformed service personnel, 7.6 million contractors, and 2.9 million grantees. This equates to a ratio of more than five "shadow" government employees for every reported civil servant on the federal payroll.

To put this in perspective, if the federal government was its own standalone country, it would be ranked 75th in the world by population. If it was a State in the Union, it would be ranked 5th among the other States.

The federal bureaucracy has been growing for decades and shows no signs of stopping. From the 1960s to the 1990s, the number of senior executives and political appointees in the federal bureaucracy quintupled, increasing the average number of layers between the president and street-level bureaucrats from 17 in 1960 to 32 in 1992. Currently, there is an average of one federal employee or contractor for every four people in the United States.

As the number of bureaucrats has increased, so have their bank accounts. Federal compensation averaged $119,934 in 2014, which was 78 percent higher than the private-sector average of $67,246.

When bureaucracy grows this large this fast, accountability is one of the first casualties. That includes accountability in accurately knowing or reporting its own size and scope. Accountability is next to non-existent in determining the actual size and scope of the federal bureaucracy. Notably, with respect to the number of agencies, the Administrative Conference of the United States—which lists 115 agencies in the appendix of its most recent Sourcebook of United States Executive Agencies—had the following to say:

"There is no authoritative list of government agencies. For example, FOIA.gov [maintained by the Department of Justice] lists 78 independent executive agencies and 174 components of the executive departments as units that comply with the Freedom of Information Act requirements imposed on every federal agency. This appears to be on the conservative end of the range of possible agency definitions. The United States Government Manual lists 96 independent executive units and 220 components of the executive departments. An even more inclusive listing comes from USA.gov, which lists 137 independent executive agencies and 268 units in the Cabinet."

To justify its existence, the federal bureaucracy constantly creates new programs within its agencies. This is where federal inefficiency is at its pinnacle. As of 2016, there were 1,158 federal programs that duplicate other programs, with substantially the same aims, covering a wide range of aims. That included 342 separate economic development programs, 130 programs serving at-risk youth, 90 early childhood development programs, 75 programs funding international education, cultural, and training exchange activities, 72 federal programs dedicated to safe water, 50 homeless assistance programs, 45 federal agencies conducting federal criminal investigations, 40 separate employment and training programs, 28 rural development programs, 27 teen pregnancy programs, 23 agencies providing aid to countries of the former Soviet Union, 19 programs fighting substance abuse, 17 rural water and waste water programs spread across 8 separate agencies, 17 trade agencies monitoring 400 international trade agreements, 12 food safety agencies, 11 principal statistics agencies, and 4 overlapping land management agencies.

The federal mentality seems to be that, if one program doesn't solve the problem, another program that does substantially the same thing should be created in addition to the one that wasn't cutting the mustard. Brian M. Riedl, a senior fellow at the Manhattan Institute, was clear on how this inefficiency is used to exponentially grow federal rules and regulations.

"This means not only additional bureaucracies to run these overlapping programs, but also an administrative nightmare for program beneficiaries who must navigate each program's distinct rules and requirements."

Since 1976, 195,189 agency rules have been issued and recorded in the *Federal Register*. The *Code of Federal Regulations* (CFR), the codified general and permanent rules and regulations of the federal government, is massive. In 1960, the CFR contained 22,877 pages. Since 1975, its total page count has grown from 71,224 to 185,053 at the end of 2016. To put it into perspective, if every page of the CFR were laid end to end, just this portion of the federal rules that govern your life would stretch more than 32 miles. Federal regulatory code currently contains more than 1 million individual regulatory restrictions. The volume of regulations is so massive that, if reading them was your full-time job, it would take you more than three years to read them all.

Of course, more regulations means more forms. Bureaucrats like paperwork. The federal government loves it. According to research from the American Action Forum (AAF), just a sample of 68 of 440 federal agencies imposes roughly 23,000 forms. These forms alone help generate more than 11.4 billion hours of paperwork annually, averaging out to 35 hours for every man, woman, and child in the United States.

Even if the federal government cannot accurately account for its true size or who works for it, it's reasonable to expect that, at a minimum, they would know the law of the land. They don't. In an example of a failed attempt to tally up the number of laws on a specific subject area, in 1982 the Justice Department launched an effort to officially identify the total number of criminal laws. It was a dismal failure. The project ended after two years without reaching a conclusion. After two years of exhaustive research, the department was able to compile a list of approximately 3,000 criminal offenses before having to throw in the towel.

The effort and its futile outcome was highlighted in a *Wall Street Journal* article, which reported that, "this effort came as part of a long and ultimately failed campaign to persuade Congress to revise the criminal code which, by the 1980s, was scattered among 50 titles and 23,000 pages of Federal law." The effort, headed by Ronald Gainer, a Justice Department official, is considered the most exhaustive attempt to count the number of federal criminal laws in history. After officially throwing in the towel, Gainer expressed his frustration. "You will have died and been resurrected three times and still not have an answer to this question."

There is a significant problem with the federal government's inability to construct a comprehensive and definitive list of criminal acts under the federal system—everyone is potentially a criminal. However, the reality is much worse than the potentiality. "There is no one in the United States over the age of 18 who cannot be indicted for some federal crime," retired Louisiana State University law professor John Baker told the *Wall Street Journal* in July 2011. "That is not an exaggeration."

A 2015 article in the *National Review* reinforced this claim. "There are so many regulations and criminal statutes on the books that a civil-liberties expert and lawyer, Harvey Silverglate, thinks that the average American commits three felonies a day, and they often are not even aware they are breaking the law. That is, not until a federal agency begins an investigation and they are indicted."

The impact of this federal superstate is being felt by Texans who find it impossible to navigate a federal rulebook under which we are required to live, but which no one can see in total. All the while, we're being crushed under the weight of a bureaucracy that continues to grow at breakneck pace but whose true size and scope are a mystery. This faceless, amorphous, uncaring bureaucracy touches and micromanages every facet of our daily lives and compels our obedience to laws they themselves do not know and cannot count, all under the threat of criminal prosecution.

NATIONAL DEBT

Bureaucracy is expensive. As Americans clamor for more programs and eschew personal responsibility by shifting it to the federal government to address every need and want, the bureaucracy grows. However, those who are the loudest to demand expansion of the federal government are the very people who don't want to pay for it. As the federal government grows, it has to increasingly spend more than it takes in. Rather than saying "no" to new programs or cutting existing programs, it does what most financially inept institutions do—it goes into debt.

The federal government is well known for its insatiable hunger for buying on credit. On September 11, 2017, while people were memorializing the 2001 terrorist attacks on New York City and the Pentagon, another devastating milestone was reached. For the first time in the history of the United States, the national debt exceeded $20 trillion.

This came as no surprise to those who have been warning about the federal debt crisis for years. In fact, this milestone was predicted by *Forbes* contributor Mike Patton in a 2015 article.

"In 2004, the Federal debt was $7.3 trillion. This rose to $10 trillion when the housing bubble burst four years later. Today it exceeds $18 trillion and is projected to approach $21 trillion by 2019."

This number is significant for a reason other than its sheer size. The Gross Domestic Product (GDP) of the United States in 2016 was $18.57 trillion. That is the total value of all goods produced and services provided in the United States for that year. To give some perspective, the United States debt-to-GDP ratio in 1980 was only 35.4 percent. By 1990, it had reached 57.7 percent. Today the amount of money owed by the federal government is 108 percent of the entire production value of the United States and climbing.

Patton's article on the debt contained a blunt warning that has been echoed by other economists and government watchdogs for many years now.

"You can be sure of this: You cannot circumvent the laws of economics. If we continue to accumulate debt, if we ignore the warning signs, if our officials maintain the status quo, there will be consequences. I only hope America realizes it before it's too late."

That warning came in 2015, yet the federal government has refused to significantly cut spending or pay down the debt. Instead, politicians, and those who support them, are proposing trillions of dollars in new spending on top of the trillions of dollars in unfunded obligations, such as Social Security.

In 2017, it was revealed that Hillary Clinton, while running for president, toyed with the idea of proposing a Universal Basic Income, wherein every single person in the United States would receive a check from the federal government simply for breathing. Her opponent in the Democratic Primary, Bernie Sanders, promised free college for all and has now introduced legislation to implement single-payer healthcare, each of these programs projected to cost trillions of dollars to implement. It's important to note that their political party received a majority of the popular vote in the 2016 election, showing the irresistible allure of "free stuff" to the majority of the people of the United States.

The spending spree is destined to end as confidence continues to wane in the federal government's ability to pay back what it owes. In 2015 and 2016, the two largest foreign holders of federal debt, Japan and China, who collectively own $2.14 trillion of the debt, began the process of reducing their holdings. They weren't the only ones. In 2015, foreign investors purchased fewer U.S. Treasuries than they sold. The year 2016 showed that it was not an aberration as foreign holdings dropped by another $201 billion.

The federal government will very soon be forced to make an impossible choice under the current system. As the total debt grows, so does the interest. The federal government has kept this system afloat by borrowing more money to pay creditors and allocating dollars in the budget to simply pay the interest on the debt. However, we are rapidly reaching a point where, just to pay the interest on the debt, services will have to be cut drastically and taxes will have to increase drastically. Social services will have to be dramatically scaled back or outright eliminated. Social Security recipients, who have been forced to pay into this alleged retirement system, will have their benefits slashed, and those who are currently paying into the system will be forced to face the fact that they have been participating in a Ponzi scheme. The defense budget will be cut to the point that the ability to protect the United States will be questionable at best. Infrastructure spending will grind to a halt, throwing federally funded roads and bridges into a greater state of disrepair. Taxes would likely have to double, throwing an already sluggish economy into a full meltdown.

The other option is that the United States could simply refuse to pay its debt. When the global debt collectors call the White House, the president could disguise his or her voice and say, "The United States doesn't live here anymore." The federal government could simply tell those holding U.S. debt to take a leap. Beyond the moral implications of such action, this path has its own set of devastating economic reper-cussions. If the surety of the ability of the United States government to pay its debts is shaken, people will stop lending money to it. This has happened before in other countries.

In a *Newsweek* column, Robert J. Samuelson laid out how this sce-nario has played out for other countries that have taken a similar route. "Deprived of domestic or international credit, defaulting countries in the past have suffered deep economic downturns, hyperinflation, or both." The effect is steep cuts in spending, a massive spike in unemployment, a severe devaluation in the dollar, and an economic depression that will make the 1930s look like a "golden age."

Make no mistake. These are actual conversations that are taking place among policymakers and actual options that are being explored. This is a sure sign that even the federal government has zero confidence that this catastrophe can be avoided.

Lest anyone feel removed or insulated from the seismic economic shifts that will occur because of the debt crisis, it is important to understand that there are real and unavoidable personal costs involved for any State that remains a member of the Union. In 2004, the individual liability for the debt was $72,051 per taxpayer. Today the per-person debt has climbed to nearly $200,000. The average annual increase is far greater than the average annual wage increase during the same timeframe. With an average median household income of $59,039 in 2016, this means that, if the debt clock stopped and the accumulation of interest was frozen, every taxpayer would still have to be taxed at 100 percent for 3.5 years to pay off the debt. That doesn't include paying for the continued operation of the federal government. To be clear, the debt clock won't stop and the interest won't be frozen because our creditors simply don't like us that much.

The national debt is a ticking time bomb that, when it explodes, will affect every man, woman, and child who is a part of this Union. That includes Texans.

THE UNEQUAL BURDEN

While it may seem that the hammer of the federal government's misdeeds hits everyone equally, it doesn't. There is evidence to show that Texans are disproportionately affected by the negative impacts of continued membership in the federal Union.

In 2014, the Mercatus Center released the Federal Regulation and State Enterprise (FRASE) Index. This index rates the level of impact federal regulations have on State economies. For 2013, Texas ranked 6th for impact of federal regulation. In fact, the impact of federal regulation on Texas industries was 29 percent higher than the impact on the United States overall. In compiling historical economic and regulatory data between 1997 and 2013, the FRASE Index has grown by 44 percent for Texas. In short, the better we do, the harder we're hit.

The largely overlooked impact of this lop-sided treatment is much more personal and felt squarely in the wallets and pocketbooks of hard-working men and women in Texas. In a 2013 study, published in the *Journal of Economic Growth*, the growth of federal regulations over the past six decades has cut U.S. economic growth by an average of 2 percentage points per year. The result is that the average household receives about $277,000 less annually than it would have gotten in the absence of sixty years of additional federal regulations. The study concluded that, without federal overregulation, the annual median household income would have been $330,000 in 2013 as opposed to the average of $53,000.

The federal government's relentless tsunami of regulations has also affected those who can least afford it—the working poor. Dr. Patrick A. McLaughlin, the director of the Program for Economic Research on Regulation and a senior research fellow at the Mercatus Center at George Mason University, put the United States Congress on notice that their relentless expansion of the federal superstate was crushing the poor and driving more into poverty. In his testimony, he cited two primary reasons why this was happening.

"First, they have regressive effects caused by increasing prices, particularly for those items that low-income households purchase most. Second, regulations can contribute to income inequality by increasing the costs of starting a business. This makes it more difficult for entrepreneurs to start their own businesses and begin the climb up the income ladder... The accumulation of regulation is both undesirable—because of a bevy of unintended consequences associated with it—and avoidable."

Although the Texas economy has managed to outpace the rest of the United States in the face of the federal government's disproportionate stifling of the Texas economy and its direct assault on the personal incomes of Texans, there is clear evidence that Texans are increasingly asked to shoulder a disproportionate share of the costs associated with the expansion of the federal government in States other than our own.

The vast majority of Texans understand that every dollar the federal government spends in Texas first comes from their pockets and that the federal government will take it any way they can get it. Whether it's the individual income tax, self-employment taxes, business income taxes, unemployment insurance taxes, estate and trust income taxes, gift taxes, excise taxes, or any other type of tax, the federal government looks at the economic prosperity of Texas like a pimp demanding money from a prostitute under his protection.

On average, Texans pay $265 billion per year in taxes to the federal government. Federal government expenditures in Texas, at best, account for only $162 billion. This is a substantial overpayment of $103 billion annually. The math is clear. Texans pay more into the federal system than we get out of it.

To put this into perspective, AIR Worldwide estimated the final price tag for Hurricane Harvey will be close to $75 billion. The amount the federal government saps out of the paychecks of Texans is the equivalent of a natural disaster the size of Harvey hitting Texas every nine months. However dramatic that figure may seem, it still doesn't tell the entire story.

The money that flows back into Texas comes in two forms. There are direct benefit payments that are not included in the figure, such as federal pension benefits and Social Security retirement. Those are obligations directly between the federal government and individuals. Another, which is included in the $162 billion, is money designated as "federal aid." The term is misleading. It is, in fact, money sent to the State for the implementation and administration of federal and federally authorized programs. In 2014, for Texas, this figure was $38.6 billion.

What isn't included in any of these figures is the cost to the Texas taxpayers for the State of Texas to implement these federal programs. That number is harder to ascertain. According to a report from the Congressional Budget Office:

"Federal grants are typically intended to supplement the efforts of state and local governments rather than supplant them. To that end, many grant programs include matching requirements or maintenance-of-effort (MOE) provisions that require state and local governments to partially pay for a program from nonfederal revenues. Some such provisions may cause state and local governments to spend more on a program than they otherwise would and may constrain their ability to spend their own revenues according to their own policy priorities. Based on the current body of economic literature, the extent to which federal grants supplant state and local spending that would have occurred anyway is unclear. That may be because the wide variety of inter-governmental programs and accompanying rules and conditions make it difficult to draw broad conclusions."

In short, the federal government takes money from Texas taxpayers and then spends it according to the priorities established by an incompetent federal bureaucracy. It then requires us to implement inefficient federal programs to be eligible to get a fraction of our tax money back. However, to do so, Texans have to pay even more tax money to the State government to be spent on the implementation of that same program. After that, we still overpay by at least $103 billion per year.

Texas has consistently been among a dozen States that pay more into the federal system than they receive. In essence, these so-called "donor states" underwrite federal spending in other States and fund the operations of the federal bureaucracy. The federal government is, naturally, less than forthcoming about where Texans' money is spent. We know that a significant chunk of it is swallowed up in the increasing costs of maintaining and expanding the federal bureaucracy.

Spending our money comes quite easily to the federal government. They are much like an unfaithful spouse who takes our paycheck and pisses it away on booze, drugs, and hookers. Lest anyone think this is an exaggeration, there is proof that our money has literally been spent on booze, drugs, and hookers. In 2009, the National Institutes of Health made headlines when it was discovered it had spent $2.6 million on a federally approved study to find out how to get prostitutes in China to cut their alcohol consumption. And, in 2013, the last year for which there are complete records, the government spent almost $1.3 million on alcohol. A government audit recently discovered that half of all purchases on government credit cards included personal mortgage payments, gambling at Vegas casinos, lingerie, XBoxes and Playstations, jewelry, Internet dating services and high-dollar luxury vacations.

Even though some of the federal spending may seem legitimate on the surface, digging deeper shows that, when the federal government needs to justify its existence, it still fails to be efficient or effective. In one two-year period, the General Accounting Office reported that just five agencies alone spent $3.1 billion on workers placed on administrative leave. The Bush administration conducted a study and found that, over a five-year period, 22 percent of all federal programs failed to show any positive impact on the populations they serve at a cost of over $123 billion annually.

Increasingly, Texans look at the wrangling over our domestic challenges like public education, property taxes, and transportation and wonder at the difference that $103 billion per year could make if it stayed in Texas. To Texans, that $103 billion wasted represents more classroom teachers, cheaper college tuition, better housing for families, money needed to start a small business, more money for charities, a more secure border, better care options for the elderly, or the elimination of onerous property taxes. In short, it represents missed opportunities to address the challenges that Texans face in the manner that Texans feel is best.

IMMIGRATION AND THE BORDER

Even with the massive taxes paid by Texans and the endless borrowing of money by the federal government, Texans still cannot get relief on their number one concern: illegal immigration and the border.

The Texas Politics Project at the University of Texas at Austin regularly polls Texans on what they feel is the most important issue facing the State. Consistently, the top two concerns are immigration and the border. When combined, it is the primary public policy concern for 31-40 percent of Texans.

To be clear, Texans are not opposed to immigration. What Texans take exception to is the federal government's approach to illegal immigration and their lack of commitment to securing the border. Texans have made it abundantly clear that they want a border with Mexico that is secure and an immigration policy that is structured, rational, and fair to those who are already citizens, as well as those who wish to become citizens. While the federal government claims that both these issues fall squarely in the scope of its authority, it has delivered none of what Texans want or need.

The federal government has been wildly inconsistent with its immigration policies and indecisive with its border policy. While the federal government fails to allocate resources to protect the border from mass illegal migration, it incentivizes those who slip through by requiring that States, including Texas, provide public services without regard to immigration status.

Texans are paying a heavy price for the federal government's stance on illegal immigration. According to a 2017 study released by the Federation for American Immigration Reform, the total net fiscal burden of illegal aliens on taxpayers is $113 billion annually. Texas taxpayers bear some of the highest costs for the virtually unrestricted mass migration, accounting for nearly $12 billion.

The impacts of U.S. border and immigration policy are felt in nearly every sphere of the public sector. Texas is ranked second in costs associated with providing in-state college tuition to illegal immigrants. Texas is one of the top four States impacted by the uncompensated medical expenses of illegal immigrants. In addition, due to the lack of commitment to border security, Texas budgets $412 million annually of its own money specifically for State-initiated border security efforts.

The lax immigration policy and the porous border have real and disturbing consequences beyond the fiscal impact. Because of the federal government's stance, there is a cost to public safety. According to the Texas Department of Public Safety, over 232,000 criminal aliens have been booked into local Texas jails between June 1, 2011 and September 30, 2017. Their criminal histories were extensive, with charges for more than 618,000 criminal offenses, including 1,256 homicide charges; 73,691 assault charges; 17,724 burglary charges; 74,112 drug charges; 746 kidnapping charges; 42,684 theft charges; 47,797 obstructing police charges; 4,051 robbery charges; 6,651 sexual assault charges; and 9,282 weapons charges. Of the total criminal aliens arrested in that timeframe, over 155,000, or 66 percent, were identified as being in the United States illegally at the time of their last arrest.

The federal government, although well aware of the challenges posed by the border and illegal immigration, seems paralyzed when it comes to actually dealing with them. Any attempt at instituting policies that would actually secure the border is stonewalled. Attempts to institute cuts or limit public services to illegal immigrants are labeled as institutional racism and unconstitutional, and are buried along with the political careers of those who proposed them.

In the face of federal inaction, Texas has tried to address these challenges through the federal system and on its own. Unilateral attempts to limit access to public services for illegal immigrants have been shot down by federal courts with stern reminders that, in the opinion of the federal government, matters related to immigration and border are under their sole authority. Texas regularly requests reimbursement from the federal government for State-initiated expenses to secure the border. To date, all requests have been denied.

Instead of plugging the holes and stemming the tide, the real drive in the federal government seems to be the exact opposite. There has been a constant theme in public discussions about these issues that the simplest solution would be to offer a shortcut to citizenship for the 11.4 million illegal immigrants that are already here and a streamlined process for those who wish to follow. The federal government has made its position clear. It values non-citizens who came here illegally more than it values citizens that it claims as its own.

AMERICA, THE IRREDEEMABLE

There are those who believe that Texas should "stick it out" and work to fix the federal government. Like small children who weep and wail at the suggestion of throwing out the remaining tatters of their safety blanket, they offer solutions that ignore reality. It is a reality expressed by author George Orwell.

"A society becomes totalitarian when its structure becomes fla-grantly artificial: that is, when its ruling class has lost its function but succeeds in clinging to power by force or fraud."

In 2011, Texas State Representative David Simpson, one of the biggest proponents of personal liberty to ever grace the halls of the Texas Capitol, attempted to push back against unconstitutional airport searches by the Transportation Safety Administration when he filed House Bill 1937.

Simpson's bill would have made it a crime for TSA agents to con-duct invasive searches during airport security screenings. That includes humiliating strip searches where TSA agents have been known to thor-oughly examine the genitalia. The bill, which would have criminal-ized "intentionally, knowingly, or recklessly touching the anus, sexual organ, buttocks, or breast of the other person, including touching through clothing, or touching the other person in a manner that would be offensive to a reasonable person." It became publicly known as the "anti-groping bill."

If an average person performed these acts, they would be classi-fied as sexual assaults and the perpetrator would spend a significant amount of time in prison. However, slap a badge and a uniform on the perpetrators, give them federal authority, claim that it's in the interest of national security, and it becomes perfectly legal.

HB 1937 passed the Texas House and was sent on to the Senate. The bill had serious momentum until the federal government responded to its passage in the House by threatening to end all air travel in Texas if it passed. As TSA officials lobbied Texas senators, and public threats from the Obama administration became more robust, the Senate sponsor, Dan Patrick, withdrew the bill with a parting shot at the wavering senators and then-Lt. Governor David Dewhurst.

"There was a time in this state, there was a time in our history, where we stood up to the federal government and we did not cower to rules and policies that invaded the privacy of Texans."

In an interview with the *Texas Tribune*, Patrick went on to say; "Our country is saying there's too much federal government in our lives, and this was a chance for Texas to take the lead and probably change the policy of TSA, because does anyone think that they're really going to close down all the airports tomorrow?"

Texas tried to push back and signal to the federal government that it was out of bounds, as it has done on many issues. The federal government doubled down and signaled to Texans that this was the totalitarian future Orwell warned us about.

The United States has found a way to further grow the bureaucracy, demand more money, and take more of our fundamental freedom. In short, the United States is becoming, or already is, a police state. In the name of national security, all citizens are now under the watchful eye of federal government surveillance and they are willing to accept any violation of their fundamental rights, most without a second thought. It is Josef Stalin's totalitarian utopia.

A certain portion of the population of the United States tries to rationalize and excuse this intrusion into our lives. National security is a legitimate concern. However, in the hands of an unaccountable bureaucracy, these rational national security concerns are amplified by naked fear mongering and transformed into an irrational acceptance of every encroachment on personal liberty and the sovereign rights of each State. That is as much the problem as the intrusion itself.

The bureaucracy has grown to the point that it has developed an existence distinct from the Union it administers. Some might liken the federal bureaucracy to a fourth branch of the federal government. The federal government is no longer subject to the people who elect representatives. It is an amalgamation of actors who, in the masquerade of a republic, work as part of a single system whose sole purpose is to enlarge the government and enrich themselves.

In Philip K. Howard's 2012 article in *The Atlantic*, he pulled no punches when calling out the federal bureaucracy and the intractable problem with fixing it.

"American government is a deviant subculture. Its leaders stand on soapboxes and polarize the public by pointing fingers while secretly doing the bidding of special interests. Many public employees plod through life with their noses in rule books, indifferent to the actual needs of the public and unaccountable to anyone. The professionals who interact with government—lawyers and lobbyists—make sure every issue is viewed through the blinders of a particular interest, not through the broader lens of the common good. Government is almost completely isolated from the public it supposedly serves. The one link that is essential for a functioning democracy—identifiable officials who have responsibility to accomplish public goals—is nowhere to be found. Who's in charge? It's hard to say. The bureaucracy is a kind of Moebius strip of passing the buck. The most powerful force in this subculture is inertia: Things happen a certain way because they happened that way yesterday. Programs are piled upon programs, without any effort at coherence; there are 82 separate federal programs, for example, for teacher training. Ancient subsidies from the New Deal are treated as sacred cows. The idea of setting priorities is anathema. Nothing can get taken away, because that would offend a special interest."

In fact, the danger posed by the federal bureaucracy has now entered the public consciousness and has been labeled "the deep state." If there is one area the "deep state" excels in, it's in protecting itself from reform. Attempts at reform have been absolute failures. While they may seem to give some short-term appearance at effectiveness and may provide catharsis for a segment of the public that wants to see the federal government fixed, in the long run it bounces back, stronger than ever.

Even the most widespread federal reform effort in recent history, the Tea Party movement, failed to identify the real issue. Clint Siegner, the director at Money Metals Exchange, was watching as the men and women of the Tea Party movement were betrayed.

"We've seen hypocrisy before. The Tea Party movement during the earlier days of the Obama administration pushed for lower taxes and less spending. Smiling Republican incumbents assured constituents they heard the message of Tea Partiers loudly and clearly. But establishment GOP lawmakers went back to Washington and stuck to business as usual. It turned out Obama was not the only impediment to downsizing the government. It was the Republican Congressional Majority who enabled every hike in the debt ceiling and ever larger federal budgets. Obama took most of the blame for the massive expansion in government, but Congress funded every penny of it. Much of the impetus behind the Tea Party has since dissipated."

In the end, the Tea Parties were betrayed because they placed their faith in a system that could not and would not be able to deliver the reforms they sincerely wanted to see. It was like sending divers to the bottom of the North Atlantic to plug the holes in the hull of the Titanic and then wondering why the ship was still inundated.

For their efforts, they were the victims of political persecution by one of the most heinous federal agencies—the Internal Revenue Service. While initially dismissed as a "crazy conspiracy theory," it is now an absolute fact that the IRS was used to target conservative and Tea Party leaders and organizations, singling them out for extensive audits and investigations. It has further been shown that they were targeted solely for their beliefs and their work to reform the federal system. The Tea Party said that the federal government was out of control. It responded by showing them exactly how out of control it really is.

When Donald Trump was elected president, the people and individuals who were targets of the IRS persecution rightly believed that, when the process began to "drain the swamp," Trump would honor his promise to fire IRS Commissioner John Koskinen. After all, while Koskinen's agency was busy persecuting conservatives and reformists, they were also busy rehiring 213 of their employees who had ducked their taxes, been convicted of theft, misused taxpayer data, and even falsified documents.

For months, House Republicans sought to impeach Koskinen for obstructing a Congressional probe into the agency's targeting of the applications for tax-exempt status made by nonprofit Tea Party organizations and conservative leaning groups.

"I don't know why President Trump hasn't fired John Koskinen since there is more evidence the agency is mismanaged," said Peter Flaherty, president of the conservative watchdog organization National Legal and Policy Center.

"Koskinen is a very typical Washington creature and is very at home in the swamp," Flaherty said in an interview with *The Daily Signal*. "It's a puzzle to me why Trump hasn't acted."

Trump never fired Koskinen. Instead, this "very Washington creature" was allowed to finish out his term with no repercussions, telling the *New York Times*, "Survival is its own reward."

Issues like these, where the federal system shows its true colors, are why fewer people than ever have faith in the federal system. In a February 2017 Gallup poll, they found that, "Dissatisfaction with the government now clearly leads as the issue Americans see as the most important problem facing the U.S."

An Allstate/Atlantic Media Heartland Monitor poll in July 2016 found that Americans think the most serious issue facing the country is that "the political system in Washington is not working well enough to produce solutions to the nation's problems."

If you thought this dissatisfaction with the federal system would translate into seeking more local and State-based solutions to issues, you'd be wrong. Another poll, this one from NBC and the *Wall Street Journal*, found that 57 percent of respondents believe the federal government "should do more to solve problems" and help people, with less than 40 percent saying that Uncle Sam is already trying to do too many things.

The paradox is obvious; in an age of widespread discontent and distrust of government institutions, most Americans still want government institutions to bite off even more than they are currently, inefficiently, and often harmfully chewing. A majority acknowledges that the federal system is terminally disconnected from the people it purports to serve. A minority has faith or trust in the institution, with even fewer believing it can be fixed. Yet a majority want it to do more, grow more, and spend more.

Guy Benson gave voice to the frustration of this paradox in an op-ed on *Townhall.com*:

"The government should deal with it, they say. But don't cut spending on anything. And don't raise taxes on anyone except "the rich," who already pay an unfair burden, according to most Americans. That's the rub: People are almost always going to demand stable or increased spending on most big programs, but also want the debt stabilized, and also don't want to personally pay for a much more expensive government through higher taxes on themselves."

For Texans, restructuring the federal government to, at a minimum, allow Texans a sliver of self-government and dignity is impossible under the current system. It boils down to simple math. Two-thirds of the States benefit from the unequal relationship between Texas and the rest of the Union. Over half of the population of the United States benefits from the federal status quo. The direction and growth of the well-entrenched bureaucracy remains set in the face of elections and partisan power shifts. Even if the composition of Congress truly mattered, Texas has 36 congressmen and 2 senators out of the 535 members of both chambers. We simply do not have the votes within the federal system to protect our interests.

Faced with the insurmountable math, some hope that Texas can lead the political equivalent of a spiritual revival and that, somehow, the ideas that make Texas great will spread to the rest of the United States in a great awakening that heralds the return to a "more perfect union." While it is true that other States may adopt our policies, the majority of the States, through generations of conditioning, are ill prepared to adopt the Texas mindset. In the end, that still doesn't address systemic problems or the political calculus that is at the core of the problems with the Union, nor does it address returning the right of self-government to the people of Texas.

This is not the Union that Texans agreed to join in 1845. It's not even the Union our fathers and their fathers knew. It's akin to joining a Christian church and watching it, over time, fundamentally change its doctrine to venerate Lucifer, the Eucharist being substituted for human sacrifice. This is not a doctrinal shift. It is a monstrous mutation. Far from being the idealized "land of milk and honey," it has become the "land of bilking money."

The cry of the Texas politician, hawking a book and seeking federal office, is that "Texas should lead the way." That presupposes that the people in the other States want a political Moses to lead them to the "Promised Land" and that the "Promised Land" is actually where they want to go. Those who want to live as Texans are already voting with their feet as record numbers are relocating to Texas and calling it home. Those who do not are staying put and voting, in record numbers, for candidates and policies that are increasingly reminiscent of Soviet collectivism.

Texans are no longer comfortable with submitting their political will to a people who, they perceive, wouldn't know liberty and good government if it jumped up and bit them in the ass. There is a precedent for this feeling in Texas. The Texas Declaration of Independence from Mexico specifically calls out the other Mexican States for their weakness in the face of Santa Anna's tyranny.

"We appealed to our Mexican brethren for assistance. Our appeal has been made in vain. Though months have elapsed, no sympathetic response has yet been heard from the Interior. We are, therefore, forced to the melancholy conclusion, that the Mexican people have acquiesced in the destruction of their liberty, and the substitution therfor of a military government; that they are unfit to be free, and incapable of self government."

Texans firmly believe the rest of America has lost its way and that Texas is more American than America. Everything that America aspired to be, Texas achieved. The personal freedom and economic opportunity envisioned by the Founders of the United States is found in Texas to a larger degree than anywhere else in the United States. While Texas is not perfect, we're working on it every single day. We may stumble and lose our way from time to time, but we always return to the path and keep moving forward.

There is no fix for the federal government using the federal government because it is the problem. It's akin to saying that the only way to put out a raging fire is to give it more oxygen and fuel. The fact remains that Texas strength makes us more resilient than most States in the face of the federal onslaught. But no State is invincible. Not even Texas.

PAST IS PROLOGUE

To put this all in perspective, it's worth looking at the problem from an old set of eyes. In 1836, the founders of the Republic of Texas were also faced with a government from a capitol far removed from them and a system that transformed the federative republic to which they had sworn loyalty into something unrecognizable. On March 2nd of that same year, they drafted and signed the Texas Declaration of Independence.

Unfortunately, few people, even in Texas, have read it. In light of what we know about the federal government, it's worth reviewing, not just by Texans but by everyone struggling to make sense out of Texit.

When a government has ceased to protect the lives, liberty and property of the people, from whom its legitimate powers are derived, and for the advancement of whose happiness it was instituted, and so far from being a guarantee for the enjoyment of those inestimable and inalienable rights, becomes an instrument in the hands of evil rulers for their oppression.

When the Federal Republican Constitution of their country, which they have sworn to support, no longer has a substantial existence, and the whole nature of their government has been forcibly changed, without their consent, from a restricted federative republic, composed of sovereign states, to a consolidated central military despotism, in which every interest is disregarded but that of the army and the priesthood, both the eternal enemies of civil liberty, the everready minions of power, and the usual instruments of tyrants.

When, long after the spirit of the constitution has departed, moderation is at length so far lost by those in power, that even the semblance of freedom is removed, and the forms them-

selves of the constitution discontinued, and so far from their petitions and remonstrances being regarded, the agents who bear them are thrown into dungeons, and mercenary armies sent forth to force a new government upon them at the point of the bayonet.

When, in consequence of such acts of malfeasance and abdication on the part of the government, anarchy prevails, and civil society is dissolved into its original elements. In such a crisis, the first law of nature, the right of self-preservation, the inherent and inalienable rights of the people to appeal to first principles, and take their political affairs into their own hands in extreme cases, enjoins it as a right towards themselves, and a sacred obligation to their posterity, to abolish such government, and create another in its stead, calculated to rescue them from impending dangers, and to secure their future welfare and happiness.

Nations, as well as individuals, are amenable for their acts to the public opinion of mankind. A statement of a part of our grievances is therefore submitted to an impartial world, in justification of the hazardous but unavoidable step now taken, of severing our political connection with the Mexican people, and assuming an independent attitude among the nations of the earth.

The Mexican government, by its colonization laws, invited and induced the Anglo-American population of Texas to colonize its wilderness under the pledged faith of a written constitution, that they should continue to enjoy that constitutional liberty and republican government to which they had been habituated in the land of their birth, the United States of America.

In this expectation they have been cruelly disappointed, inasmuch as the Mexican nation has acquiesced in the late changes made in the government by General Antonio Lopez de Santa Anna, who having overturned the constitution of his country, now offers us the cruel alternative, either to abandon our homes, acquired by so many privations, or submit to the most intolerable of all tyranny, the combined despotism of the sword and the priesthood.

It has sacrificed our welfare to the state of Coahuila, by which our interests have been continually depressed through a jealous and partial course of legislation, carried on at a far distant seat of government, by a hostile majority, in an unknown tongue, and this too, notwithstanding we have petitioned in the humblest terms for the establishment of a separate state government, and have, in accordance with the provisions of the national constitution, presented to the general Congress a republican constitution, which was, without just cause, contemptuously rejected.

It incarcerated in a dungeon, for a long time, one of our citizens, for no other cause but a zealous endeavor to procure the acceptance of our constitution, and the establishment of a state government.

It has failed and refused to secure, on a firm basis, the right of trial by jury, that palladium of civil liberty, and only safe guarantee for the life, liberty, and property of the citizen.

It has failed to establish any public system of education, although possessed of almost boundless resources, (the public domain,) and although it is an axiom in political science, that unless a people are educated and enlightened, it is idle to expect the continuance of civil liberty, or the capacity for self government.

It has suffered the military commandants, stationed among us, to exercise arbitrary acts of oppression and tyranny, thus trampling upon the most sacred rights of the citizens, and rendering the military superior to the civil power.

It has dissolved, by force of arms, the state Congress of Coahuila and Texas, and obliged our representatives to fly for their lives from the seat of government, thus depriving us of the fundamental political right of representation.

It has demanded the surrender of a number of our citizens, and ordered military detachments to seize and carry them into the Interior for trial, in contempt of the civil authorities, and in defiance of the laws and the constitution.

It has made piratical attacks upon our commerce, by commissioning foreign desperadoes, and authorizing them to seize our vessels, and convey the property of our citizens to far distant ports for confiscation.

It denies us the right of worshipping the Almighty according to the dictates of our own conscience, by the support of a national religion, calculated to promote the temporal interest of its human functionaries, rather than the glory of the true and living God.

It has demanded us to deliver up our arms, which are essential to our defence, the rightful property of freemen, and formidable only to tyrannical governments.

It has invaded our country both by sea and by land, with intent to lay waste our territory, and drive us from our homes;

and has now a large mercenary army advancing, to carry on against us a war of extermination.

It has, through its emissaries, incited the merciless savage, with the tomahawk and scalping knife, to massacre the inhabitants of our defenseless frontiers.

It hath been, during the whole time of our connection with it, the contemptible sport and victim of successive military revolutions, and hath continually exhibited every characteristic of a weak, corrupt, and tyrannical government.

These, and other grievances, were patiently borne by the people of Texas, untill they reached that point at which forbearance ceases to be a virtue. We then took up arms in defence of the national constitution. We appealed to our Mexican brethren for assistance. Our appeal has been made in vain. Though months have elapsed, no sympathetic response has yet been heard from the Interior. We are, therefore, forced to the melancholy conclusion, that the Mexican people have acquiesced in the destruction of their liberty, and the substitution therfor of a military government; that they are unfit to be free, and incapable of self government.

The necessity of self-preservation, therefore, now decrees our eternal political separation.

We, therefore, the delegates with plenary powers of the people of Texas, in solemn convention assembled, appealing to a candid world for the necessities of our condition, do hereby resolve and declare, that our political connection with the Mexican nation has forever ended, and that the people of Texas do now constitute a free, Sovereign, and independent republic, and are fully invested with all the rights and attri-

butes which properly belong to independent nations; and, conscious of the rectitude of our intentions, we fearlessly and confidently commit the issue to the decision of the Supreme arbiter of the destinies of nations.

4 | PROJECT FEAR

> **"**The hopes of the usurper were inspired by a belief that the citizens of Texas were disunited and divided in opinion; that alone has been the cause of the present invasion of our rights. He shall realize the fallacy of his hopes in the union of her citizens, and their Eternal Resistance to his plans against constitutional liberty. We will enjoy our birthright, or perish in its defence.**"**
>
> *Proclamation of Sam Houston, A Call for Volunteers,*
> *December 12, 1835*

In September of 2014, the people of Scotland went to the polls to determine their future by answering one simple question.

"Should Scotland be an independent country?"

Centuries of longing for independence and decades of successful political struggle had been reduced to six words on a piece of paper. The simplicity of the question betrayed the complexity behind the decision each Scot was being asked to make.

In the years ahead of the actual vote, the issue was hotly debated. The Scottish National Party had included the referendum as a major part of their election manifesto in the two previous general elections and worked hard to make good on the promise.

When the legal wrangling was over and a date for the referendum was set, two official campaigns emerged. Yes Scotland! in favor of independence and Better Together in favor of remaining a part of the United Kingdom. On the first anniversary of the launch of the Better Together campaign, the *Sunday Herald* newspaper claimed, "Privately, some inside Better Together even refer to the organisation as Project Fear." The name came from the acknowledgement that the primary tactic of Better Together was scaremongering.

Indeed, fear is the favorite tactic of those in power who wish to motivate people to take a specific action or, in the case of Scotland and Texas, prevent them from asserting independence.

Project Fear arguments, in regard to Texit, tend to fall into one of three broad categories:

"Texit is illegal."

"They won't let us."

"Texit is too hard."

Gathered together into a single statement, the total argument flows along these lines:

"Texas can't leave the union because it's illegal and unconstitutional. The Civil War settled it. Therefore, if Texas tried, the federal government would never let us. Even if it wasn't illegal, we are far too integrated with the United States, making it impossible to leave. But, even if we were to somehow magically pull it off, we're simply not big enough or strong enough outside of the United States to be successful. We'd be bankrupt in 10 years and begging the United States to let us back in."

The tenor of these arguments represents the fundamental problem with the vast majority of objections raised by Texit opponents. When the Texas version of Project Fear is confronted with facts and logic that concretely rebut its arguments or information that throws its conclusions and assumptions into question, it ignores the result and shifts to a different argument. Unable to keep its arguments from being shot down, the Project Fear strategy can be summed up in one sentence: "Scare them as much as possible, as often as possible, and, if you keep moving, they'll eventually miss."

TEXIT IS ILLEGAL AND UNCONSTITUTIONAL

A common accusation by those opposed to Texit is that the act of leaving the Union is illegal. Let's be clear. An accusation of the commission of an illegal act implies that those committing it are criminals guilty of a criminal act. Therefore, this is not a light accusation.

When pressed, however, no one seems to be able to point to a specific law that forbids it. Scouring the federal statutes produces no joy for the accuser as there is no law that explicitly forbids any State from asserting its independence. Given the passion with which this accusation is leveled, if it is not found in federal law, then surely it must exist in Texas statute. After all, the State of Nevada included one of the most strongly worded prohibitions on secession in its state constitution.

"But the Paramount Allegiance of every citizen is due to the Federal Government in the exercise of all its Constitutional powers as the same have been or may be defined by the Supreme Court of the United States; and no power exists in the people of this or any other State of the Federal Union to dissolve their connection therewith or perform any act tending to impair, subvert, or resist the Supreme Authority of the government of the United States."

However, there is no corresponding constitutional or statutory prohibition in Texas law, either.

It is a fundamental principle of American jurisprudence that something is illegal only if there is a law forbidding it. This is known as the legality principle, expressed in Latin as "nullum crimen sine lege, nulla poena sine lege," meaning "no crime without law, nor punishment without law."

Paul H. Robinson, one of the world's leading criminal law scholars, described its modern application in 2005.

"In its modern form it means that criminal liability and punishment can be based only upon a prior legislative enactment of a prohibition that is expressed with adequate precision and clarity. The principle is not a legal rule, but rather a legal concept embodied in a series of legal doctrines."

If no law specifically prohibits a State from leaving the Union, then there must be some other law which, in their minds, applies in this instance. When pressed further, the accusation shifts to that of treason.

The term "treason" has become an increasingly popular charge in this divisive political climate. While Texit advocates are the recipients of it at a higher than average rate, it has become far more common in federal partisan wrangling. Obama was accused of treason over the Iran nuclear deal and Trump has been accused of treason for his alleged ties to the Russian government. However, those who seem to be quickest to use the term seem to be most clueless as to its meaning.

Drawing from an English statute from 1351 that was created to limit the scope of treason, the framers of the United States Constitution included a specific definition in Article 3, Section 3, which stated that, "Treason against the United States shall consist only in levying war against them, or in adhering to their enemies, giving them aid and comfort."

Recognizing that accusations of treason were often the tool of tyrants, James Madison explained the necessity to clearly define it in Federalist 43.

"As treason may be committed against the United States the authority of the United States ought to be enabled to punish it: but as new tangled and artificial treasons have been the great engines by which violent factions, the natural offspring of free governments, have usually wreaked their alternate malignity on each other, the Convention has with great judgment opposed a barrier to this peculiar danger by inserting a Constitutional definition of the crime."

Treason is a criminal act committed by an individual, not a political body and, therefore, cannot be committed by a State. To continue to level the charge of treason, one must believe that the entirety of the population of Texas who would vote in support of Texit would be individually guilty of treason. This, however, completely ignores the constitutional definition of treason.

Such a vote is not levying war against the United States unless one considers casting a ballot as an act of war. Nor is it adhering to or giving aid and comfort to an enemy of the United States. If so, who would that enemy be? An enemy of the United States is someone who has been declared as such by the United States Congress, generally through a formal declaration of war. In this instance, North Korea might perhaps fit the bill, since the Korean War was never formally concluded.

According to Carlton F.W. Larson, a professor of law at the University of California at Davis, "Certain nonstate actors can also count as enemies, and terrorist groups such as al-Qaeda and the Islamic State probably fit the definition."

Adhering to the enemy would mean that voting for Texit was, in fact, joining North Korea or the Islamic State. Giving aid and comfort would mean that voting for Texit was, in fact, providing concrete and material support to the same. Neither of these apply.

When confronted with the lack of basis for the charge of treason, the final charge is that of attempting to overthrow the government. In fairness, there is a federal statute in Title 18 of the U.S. Code that outlaws attempts to do that very thing. In its entirety, it reads:

"Whoever knowingly or willfully advocates, abets, advises, or teaches the duty, necessity, desirability, or propriety of overthrowing or destroying the government of the United States or the government of any State, Territory, District or Possession thereof, or the government of any political subdivision therein, by force or violence, or by the assassination of any officer of any such government; or

Whoever, with intent to cause the overthrow or destruction of any such government, prints, publishes, edits, issues, circulates, sells, distributes, or publicly displays any written or printed matter advocating, advising, or teaching the duty, necessity, desirability, or propriety of overthrowing or destroying any government in the United States by force or violence, or attempts to do so; or

Whoever organizes or helps or attempts to organize any society, group, or assembly of persons who teach, advocate, or encourage the overthrow or destruction of any such government by force or violence; or becomes or is a member of, or affiliates with, any such society, group, or assembly of persons, knowing the purposes thereof

Shall be fined under this title or imprisoned not more than twenty years, or both, and shall be ineligible for employment by the United States or any department or agency thereof, for the five years next following his conviction."

The operative words in the statute are "force or violence" and, given that a Texit, initiated by a legal process, ratified by a vote of the people of Texas, and secured by a declaration of the reclamation of the right of self-determination, is neither force nor violence, this accusation falls as well.

Once the argument of illegality lies in ruins, the fallback position is to loudly declare that it is unconstitutional for a State to leave the Union. However, the accusation of unconstitutionality shares a fundamental and fatal flaw with the accusation of illegality. There is not a single clause in the Constitution of the United States that forbids Texas, or any State, for that matter, from leaving the Union. In this case, the constitutional silence is extremely important.

The Constitution of the United States, actually defines the specific acts States are forbidden from committing in Article 1, Section 10.

"No State shall enter into any Treaty, Alliance, or Confederation; grant Letters of Marque and Reprisal; coin Money; emit Bills of Credit; make any Thing but gold and silver Coin a Tender in Payment of Debts; pass any Bill of Attainder, ex post facto Law, or Law impairing the Obligation of Contracts, or grant any Title of Nobility.

"No State shall, without the Consent of the Congress, lay any Imposts or Duties on Imports or Exports, except what may be absolutely necessary for executing its inspection Laws: and the net Produce of all Duties and Imposts, laid by any State on Imports or Exports, shall be for the Use of the Treasury of the United States; and all such Laws shall be subject to the Revision and Control of the Congress.

"No State shall, without the Consent of Congress, lay any duty of Tonnage, keep Troops, or Ships of War in time of Peace, enter into any Agreement or Compact with another State, or with a foreign Power, or engage in War, unless actually invaded, or in such imminent Danger as will not admit of delay."

Nowhere in the remainder of the Constitution is the issue of a State leaving the Union explicitly forbidden, nor is power ceded to the federal government to prohibit one from doing so. In this silence, the Tenth Amendment to the Constitution rings loudly.

"The powers not delegated to the United States by the Constitution, nor prohibited by it to the States, are reserved to the States respectively, or to the people."

This deafening constitutional silence, coupled with the definitive reservation of power by the States, leaves the decision to the people of a State and to those people alone.

"Not so fast!" say the critics. "What about the Supreme Court case of Texas v. White? Didn't that say that secession was unconstitutional?"

The entire legal argument for the unconstitutionality of States leaving the Union rests on the Supreme Court's decision in the 1869 case of Texas v. White. However, when it comes to Texas v. White, more and more academics are adopting the stance of historian Dr. Brion McClanahan. When asked that very question at an academic conference in Florida, his response was an indignant, "So what?"

Dr. McClanahan's attitude toward Texas v. White is not based on a denial of facts. In fact, contrary to the concrete pronouncements by Texit detractors, the decision in Texas v. White has been debated and debunked extensively starting from the moment Chief Justice Salmon P. Chase issued the majority opinion.

The dissenting opinion, issued by Justice Robert C. Grier, highlighted many of the deficiencies of the Supreme Court's ruling, stating that he disagreed "on all points raised and decided." The assertions made by Chase were so offensive to his contemporaries that Union and Confederate sympathizers, both fresh from the battlefields and still harboring deep divisions, were united in their contempt for his ruling.

Bristling at the usurpation by the judiciary of the power to determine political questions, Lyman Trumbull, a United States senator from Illinois, introduced legislation that, in part, stated, "Under the Constitution, the judicial power of the United States does not embrace political power, or give to judicial tribunals any authority to question the political departments of the Government on political questions."

There is no doubt that Chief Justice Chase, an appointee of Abraham Lincoln, used the opportunity presented by Texas v. White to stamp a retroactive "seal of approval" on the federal government's policies and actions during the Civil War. To do so, Chase had to rewrite history and virtually all established law on the subject.

To reinforce his belief that the United States was a "perpetual union," he had to assert the ludicrous argument that the United States Constitution was merely an amending document to the previous Articles of Confederation, citing the Preamble to the Constitution. He then had to ignore that it only took 9 States of the original 13 to ratify the Constitution of 1787 and that, had less than 13 States ratified, it would have destroyed the "perpetual union" allegedly created by the Articles of Confederation.

To reinforce his assertion that the United States was an "indestructible Union, composed of indestructible States," Chase had to ignore the existence of West Virginia, and the agreement with the Republic of Texas upon its admission, that it could divide into 4 additional States and that those additional States would be guaranteed admission into the Union if they so chose.

To reinforce his assertion that States, upon entering the Union, gave up all rights of sovereignty and became incorporated in a single, monolithic superstate, Chase had to ignore every reference to the States as individual political entities in the Declaration of Independence, the aforementioned Articles of Confederation, the Northwest Ordinance, the United States Constitution, and all intent of the framers, clearly expressed in the period.

In his zeal to confirm the supremacy of the Union, Chase ascribed qualities to it that are usually reserved for deities. In effect, he equated the Union to God and established a quasi-religious orthodoxy that requires adherence to a doctrine that elevates the federal government to godhood, its three branches to the Holy Trinity, and the judiciary as its holy priesthood.

There is no doubt that, had the States been exposed to Chase's logic during deliberations over the ratification of the Constitution, they would have soundly rejected it and likely drafted a new Declaration of Independence.

The Supreme Court was not and never will be perfect. Some of the most heinous, morally reprehensible, logically flawed decisions have emanated from the Supreme Court. To imbue it with infallibility is to say that, when it upheld slave catching or when it upheld racial segregation, it was right. Yet decisions by the Court in both of those instances have been overturned.

Even Supreme Court Justice Oliver Wendell Holmes, Jr., in the 1904 case of Northern Securities Co. v. United States, recognized that the Court could be caught up in the politics and passions of the day and render bad decisions.

"Great cases like hard cases make bad law. For great cases are called great, not by reason of their importance... but because of some accident of immediate overwhelming interest which appeals to the feelings and distorts the judgment."

With all its obvious flaws, some academics continue to point to Texas v. White as the "silver bullet" that handles all questions related to States separating from the Union. However, others tend to glide over it so as not to have to acknowledge its most significant problem. Embracing Texas v. White requires one to believe the last 150 years never happened.

Since 1869, the world kept spinning. Generations have come and gone, and the Supreme Court has continued to issue rulings that chip away at the foundations of Texas v. White. As the entirety of Chase's determination is predicated on the claim that "perpetual union" is the "more perfect union" spoken of in the Preamble of the Constitution, the single ruling by the Court in the 1905 case of Jacobson v. Massachusetts, where it was determined that the federal government can gain no powers based on the Preamble, could utterly destroy Texas v. White.

The federal government's position on self-determination has evolved to the point of signing international agreements, covenants, and treaties pledging to respect the right of self-determination. The same chorus of voices who declare that Texas v. White is the "end all, be all" of decisions on the matter of self-determination of the States are the same voices who declare that subsequent rulings by the Supreme Court obligate the federal government and the States to give treaty obligations, such as those dealing with self-determination, the same weight as constitutional law and argue for its application as such.

Ultimately, though, any question of self-determination is political in nature. It is not, and never will be, a judicial question. Perhaps recognizing this fact and hoping to avoid any serious examination of the constitutionality of the question in general and Texas v. White specifically, those opposed to Texit quickly move on to their next argument.

Justice Antonin Scalia is often cited using the next argument. Taken from a letter written to an aspiring screenwriter, Scalia declared, "If there was any constitutional issue resolved by the Civil War, it is that there is no right to secede."

This is also a sentiment echoed by Paul Finkelman, a senior fellow in the Penn Program on Democracy, Citizenship and Constitutionalism at the University of Pennsylvania and a scholar-in-residence at the National Constitution Center, in a 2015 column in the *New York Times*.

"In short, nullification and secession were not new ideas in 1861, when 11 states left the Union, but had been part of the warp and weft of constitutional debate since the founding. But the Civil War ended the discussion. The question of the constitutionality of nullification or secession was permanently settled by the 'legal case' of Lee v. Grant, decided at Appomattox Court House in April 1865."

This refrain is echoed more often than any other and is where fear truly enters into the strategy of Project Fear. It is a quick retort that is meant to stifle all further debate on the issue through intimidation. Let's be honest. The assertions of the illegality or constitutionality of a State leaving the Union and that the Civil War settled the issue, although often linked, are truly two separate and distinct arguments. The former deals with a point of law that can be discussed, debated, and a definitive conclusion reached. The latter is a thinly veiled threat of violence, often used as a tactic by bullies, abusers of women and children, and tin-pot dictators propping up tyrannical regimes.

However, this argument also poses a significant legal, political, and moral problem for the United States and the world. If the military conquest of the States that seceded during the 1860s was the point at which the question of leaving the Union was settled, does this mean that all political questions, especially those related to self-determination, are deemed as perpetually solved by the use of force?

In a larger geopolitical sense, think about how that principle would have played out in the 20th century. When Germany invaded Poland, touching off the Second World War, how much different would the world be if the response from the United States was, "I guess that settles that." Or Japan's successful invasion of the Philippines. MacArthur's response was, "I shall return." It wasn't, "It is now settled that the Philippines are now an indivisible and inseparable part of the Empire of Japan."

Advocates of this line of thinking are missing the forest for the trees. If the Civil War truly did settle this issue, then no one would even be discussing it. It would be a fact. Establishment politicians, academia, and the media throw around the word "consensus" as though "everyone" agrees that the Civil War settled the issue and that anyone who disagrees is an outlier.

Take, for instance, Harvey Tucker, political science professor at Texas A&M, whose position on the matter has been parroted by other professors and regurgitated by a lazy media. According to Tucker, "Among scholars, the consensus is that the Civil War settled all these issues. Texas does not have the right to secede."

Tucker, and those like him, ignore the ongoing scholarship on the issue and instead opt for a sound bite followed by a definitive declaration. The media largely ignores the numerous academic conferences held over the last 20 years dealing with the right of secession, the impact of international law on the right of self-determination, and the constitutional history of secession, many of them taking place in the United States with notable U.S. scholars. If the Civil War definitively and decisively settled the issue of separation from the Union, apparently the larger academic community didn't get the memo.

The Texit question, though, is not one that is left solely to academics and their discussions of political and legal theory. What matters most on this political question is not whether the Civil War settled it, but whether the people of Texas believe that a question was settled that they've never been properly asked. The growth of support for Texit clearly shows that fewer and fewer Texans consider the result of the Civil War the final answer to the independence question.

THE FEDERAL GOVERNMENT
WON'T LET TEXAS LEAVE

There is little doubt that the federal government and its supporters will spend enormous sums of money lobbying against giving Texans even a vote on independence. When it reaches the ballot, they will spend even more in an actual campaign, trying to persuade Texans that Texit will bring certain calamity. If they fail in that, what recourse do they have?

When all arguments fail, the fallback is the threat of creating a sequel to the American Civil War—Civil War 2: America Harder. It is interesting to note that, in recent years, as the federal government has had to comment on the issue of Texit, no elected official has ever made this threat. The Obama White House, in its official response to the 2012 Texit petition, never threatened the use of force to keep Texas in the Union. While they did invoke the Civil War, it was done as a gateway to invoking the Supreme Court decision in Texas v. White. In fact, when Donald Trump was asked about Texit in 2016, he declared that Texas' love for him would keep us in.

Instead, it's the federal apologists who throw out their "apocalypse porn" version of how events would unfold.

"If Texas leaves, the federal government will empty out Fort Hood, arrest the Texas government, and shoot everyone who voted for independence."

Don't laugh. Some form of that statement has been sincerely offered by many of those opposed to Texit. Most publicly, it was uttered in a debate by a member of the Texas State Republican Executive Committee while speaking in opposition to placing a non-binding Texit question on the primary ballot. This came from a man whose party reveres President Ronald Reagan for his call to the Soviet Union to respect the right of self-determination for the countries behind the Iron Curtain. "Mister Gorbachev, tear down that wall."

Often, though, those who tender this argument are the same crowd that wants to reshape U.S. domestic policy to look more like Europe. However, in modern-day Europe, there is not a single example to show Europe has a thirst to use military power to override self-determination on the continent. There are no examples of the British threatening to use force to keep Scotland in the U.K. ahead of Scotland's 2014 independence referendum, and there has been no mobilization of troops on the European continent preparing to invade Britain in the wake of the Brexit vote. Indeed, those who are quickest to jump to the conclusion that Texit would invite a military invasion by the federal government are some of the harshest critics of U.S. military interventions around the world.

When we hear this excuse from non-Texans, it is delivered with a harshness that betrays a deep-seated desire to simply wipe Texas off the map. When it's heard from Texans, it's with a meekness more befitting Moses Rose, the only man who, according to legend, fled the Alamo, than to the heroes of the Texas Revolution. Either way, it is another fantastical scenario used to avoid serious discussion and debate on the merits of independence, a debate these Texans feel sure they will lose.

One cannot reasonably assume that the policy of the federal government from the mid-19th century would be the policy of the federal government two decades into the 21st. There is no current federal policy regarding a State leaving the Union. However, there is current federal policy regarding states and territories leaving currently established political and economic institutions. Those policies involve neutrality or the use of military action in support of self-determination.

Imagine the scenario. Fifteen million Texans have gone to the polls and voted in a free, fair, and open referendum, conducted under the laws of the State of Texas, and have chosen, by a majority vote, to leave the Union and assert Texas' status as a free and independent self-governing nation-state. Historically, around the world, voter turnout for independence referenda is 85 to 90 percent. Taking the low end, that would mean that 12.75 million Texans would cast their vote in the referendum. Figuring the lowest possible threshold for an independence victory, approximately 6.4 million Texans would vote in favor of independence.

If the federal government opts for a military solution, how would it handle the 6.4 million Texans who voted in favor of independence? Prison? Extermination? What would the justification be for any actions taken against Texans whose sole crime was voting for self-determination in a fair, free, and open referendum? When exactly would this military intervention occur? Would they do it before a vote on Texit to prevent the people having their say? Would they wait until after the results of the vote were tallied and the results announced in favor of independence? Or would they wait until after Texas began the process of extracting itself from the federal system and began asserting its role as a nation among nations?

Under close scrutiny, it becomes apparent that the federal government will not move to stop Texit once it's been decided by the people of Texas and they most certainly won't use the military. It's just too impractical.

First, there would be little to no public support for military action against Texans who voted to leave the Union. A 2011 IBOPE Zogby poll found that 43 percent of respondents believed that States had justification for leaving the Union. For those who consider themselves conservatives, that number jumps to 65 percent. Military action against Texas, in the absence of some morally reprehensible act, would require a strong consensus from the remaining States and the people in those

States. The strong liberal States would likely fall on the side of letting Texas go. The strong conservative States would be split on the issue but would largely be supportive of the basic principle of self-government. With numbers like these, a consensus seems implausible.

The use of military force would bring a swift condemnation from the international community and would damage international relations for years to come. Some countries would likely impose economic sanctions on the United States until the civilian government of Texas was restored and the results of the independence vote respected. It would also cause a tectonic shift in international policy related to the support of democratic institutions, essentially delegitimizing any efforts made by the United States past, present, and future.

You would have to believe that troops would obey an order to fire on millions of Texas civilians and their leaders whose only crime was invoking their right of self-government. With approximately 170,000 Texans serving in the United States armed forces, it would be difficult to get compliance. The ultimate irony is that any Texan in the United States military who took up arms against the lawfully elected government of Texas or its citizens would be guilty of treason under Article 1, Section 22 of the Texas Constitution.

A 2009 poll from the aforementioned Zogby poll showed a large number of military personnel and their families believed that States had an absolute right to leave the Union. As published in *Forbes*, "42% of members of the armed forces and 41% of people who have a family member active in the armed forces agree secession is a right..." The fact that 42 percent view it as a right carries weight. It means they view it as a fundamental freedom, like freedom of speech and freedom of religion. Just as it is unlikely that the military would act against those rights when exercised by the civilian population, it is equally unlikely that they would act against Texit.

The most likely scenario, if an order of this nature was given, would be outright disobedience from the highest levels of the military all the way down to the enlisted ranks by at least 42 percent of the military, if not all. If some component of the military followed through on the order, it would likely trigger a domino effect where other States, outraged by the disregard for the political will of the people of Texas, would skip to the end of the process and unilaterally declare independence. Texas might be the first to leave but, if the federal government used the military to suppress the result, it certainly would not be the last.

Although the lack of public support and the impracticality of military action are significant factors, the real reason the federal government won't stop Texas from leaving the Union is one of the most biggest drivers of federal policy—economics.

Economies hate disruption. Texit would no doubt be disruptive, but it comes down to what is more disruptive. Ordering military intervention would be economically disruptive and would create shockwaves throughout the U.S. and global economies. Carrying out any type of military intervention would be even worse. The best course of action for the United States would be to mitigate disruption in the most practical way it can—at the negotiating table. It is the most practical choice open to the federal government in dealing with a successful Texit vote.

To illustrate the oversized role that practicality plays in this arena, one only needs to look at the statements from the federal government on Brexit. In his now infamous visit to the U.K., President Obama told the British people that, if they voted to leave the European Union, the United States would place the U.K. at the "back of the queue" in negotiating a trade deal. The British people voted to leave the European Union anyway. Now the federal government is currently at the table with the U.K., laying the groundwork for a trade deal. When faced with the choice of irrationally shunning the world's fifth largest economy, with a GDP only $1 trillion greater than Texas or rationally executing a trade deal, the federal government chose the practical route.

It is far easier to negotiate a free trade agreement with a Texas that's on its way out the door than it is to militarily occupy its capital in Austin. It is easier to negotiate a currency union with Texas than it is to deal with the possibility of massive insubordination in your military. With a negotiated separation, the federal government has the opportunity to show that it believes in the principles that it has espoused around the world for the last 70 years. It is better to keep goods and services flowing than to have them come to a dead stop. Forced integration into the Union at the point of a gun invites international condemnation and the loss of credibility on the international stage for the next 70 years.

TEXIT IS TOO DIFFICULT

There are some out there who, not really understanding Texans, offer the final and, frankly, weakest arguments against Texit.

"Texas is too integrated with the United States so it's impossible to separate. If Texas does manage to separate, we'd never make it on our own."

It is true that Texas is highly integrated with the United States. However, these political and economic ties are not so tight or intricately interwoven that it would be impossible to untangle them. In many instances, it would not be necessary to untangle them at all. There is no part of the relationship between Texas and the rest of the United States that could not be accomplished by utilizing existing State-level institutions and agencies, executing bilateral agreements between Texas and the United States, or by Texas signing onto multilateral international agreements that are already in place.

Is the issue trade? Countries, including the United States, trade with one another every hour of every day and have done so for all of recorded human history. The free trade agreements that the United States already has in place for 20 other countries around the world treat trade with them as though they were one of the States of the Union. Yet no one would argue that any of those countries are inseparable members of the federal Union. Texas could execute a free trade agreement with the United States and adopt the United States tariff schedule with the World Trade Organization for external trade, and no one would even notice the difference.

Is the issue currency? If Texas needed or wanted to, it could adopt the U.S. dollar as its official currency in an informal currency union like many other countries have done. We don't need permission to do it. However, if Texas were so inclined and the United States were amenable, we could enter into an official currency union with the United States. Scotland proposed a similar move for itself and the United Kingdom ahead of its independence vote. This would be similar to the formal currency union that exists throughout the European Union.

Is the issue banking? Foreign banks are allowed to operate in the United States at this very moment with no trouble. That includes large retail banks like Compass and HSBC. In fact, more banks in Texas are state-chartered and state-regulated than those that are federally chartered and regulated.

Is the issue federal pension benefits? People live outside of the United States and collect their federal pensions, including Social Security, every month. The Social Security Administration has an entire section on its website and publishes numerous informational documents on this subject. Through totalization agreements with other countries, U.S. citizens work outside the United States and continue to pay into the United States Social Security system and vice versa.

Is the issue travel? Cars, planes, trucks, and trains move between the United States and other countries every day. Over 1 million people per day legally cross the border between the United States and Mexico for work or travel using only a "Border Crossing Card." No passport needed. This is essentially no different than traveling between Texas and Oklahoma, Louisiana, or New Mexico.

Perhaps the concerns are more about having the money to continue certain functions of government. Not a problem. Simple arithmetic proves the ability of an independent Texas to fund a government at the same level that Texans are currently accustomed to if that's what Texans want.

Texans currently pay, in all, federal and state taxes of $336 billion per year. This represents the total amount of revenue readily available to an independent Texas without increasing the financial burden on Texans one single cent. From that amount, subtract the amount spent by both the federal government and state government in Texas. $228 billion is the total amount of expenditures required to maintain every program, every job (both civilian and military), every department, every facility (including military bases) and fulfill every function (including current federal contract spending to Texas companies) provided by the federal and state governments. This level of government revenue would rank Texas 12th in the world for government revenue collected.

Somehow, since 1945, 140 new, formerly dependent countries have been able to "make it" as independent, self-governing nation-states. The unspoken assertion is that, to be able to do anything that Texas would have to do as an independent nation, it must be a part of the United States. The implication is that Texas, and Texans, aren't as good, as smart, or as capable as other nations.

This requires them to ignore the truth about how Texas stacks up against other self-governing countries in the world. In every category in which nation-states are traditionally compared, Texas overperforms.

- Texas has the 10th largest economy in the world.

- Texas ranks 40th in the world in size.

- Texas ranks 47th in the world in population.

- Texas ranks 40th in the world in the size of its labor force.

- Texas is a net global exporter ranking 22nd in the world, leading all other States in the United States.

- 93 percent of Texas exports are manufactured exports.

- Texas is the 12th largest technology exporter in the world.

- Texas ranks 19th in the world in the size of its active farms and ranches.

- Texas is the largest energy producer in the United States, accounting for more than half of the entire United States energy production and one-quarter of the refining capacity with over 26 petroleum refineries.

- Texas has the 7th largest coal reserves.

- Texas is the 6th largest producer of wind energy in the world.

- Texas has its own power grid.

These statistics, while impressive, don't tell the whole story. Texas not only does well in spite of the federal government, Texas is already structurally capable of doing everything that is traditionally done by a national government. In Texas, you will also find a state-level analog for every single cabinet-level federal department.

Texas even has its own military. The Texas Military Department is composed of the three branches of the military in the State of Texas. These branches are the Texas Army National Guard, the Texas Air National Guard, and the Texas State Guard. All three branches are administered by the state adjutant general, an appointee of the governor of Texas, and fall under the command of the Texas governor. The State Guard, which is exclusively under the command of the governor, is divided into six army regiments, two air wings, three maritime regiments, and three medical battalions. The Texas Army National Guard consists of the 36th Infantry Division, 71st Troop Command, and the 176th Engineering Brigade. The Texas Air National Guard consists of the 149th Fighter Wing, 147th Attack Wing, and the 136th Airlift Wing.

Contrary to the opinion of some, Texas' attachment to the federal system is not a special case. There was no union in recent history with more power aggregated into a central government than the Soviet Union. Within an even tighter integration and under extreme economic stress, its constituent republics were able to extract themselves and become fully functioning nation-states. If the United States has truly become more centrally controlled than the Soviet Union, then it is no longer the United States. It has become the United State and no longer represents the vision of its founders.

If those who believe that separation is too difficult are to be believed, and today it is too complicated, tomorrow it will be more so and the day after harder still. If this argument is true, then Texas is destined to fall ever deeper into the depths of the federal system until Texas is only a distant memory that exists in a history book.

It is a false argument and one that strikes counter to everything Texans have historically believed about themselves. It runs contrary to the reputation gained by Texans around the world. It is the same argument made by "helicopter parents" for why their children should still live at home well into their thirties. And it's the excuse used by socially stunted adults, well into their thirties, as to why they still live with mommy and daddy.

Ultimately, Texans bristle at the suggestion that we simply aren't good enough to govern ourselves. We reject the idea that independence can't be done as we remember the old adage that, "If you want something done, tell a Texan that it can't be done."

The real question is this: Given all our natural advantages, if Texas can't make it as an independent nation, then who can?

THE FALL OF PROJECT FEAR

In 2016, Republican supporters of Texit were standing up in county conventions all over Texas to fight for a vote on the issue. But, in Jefferson County, the debate took a fiery turn when independence supporters were accused of being criminals.

During the debate on the Texas Independence Resolution, which called for a vote on Texas reasserting its status as an independent nation, one pro-federal Republican took his opportunity to accuse all Texit supporters of the crime of sedition.

Unfortunately for him, one of the delegates to the Jefferson County convention was me. Using Robert's Rules of Order, I immediately called a point of order and demanded an apology.

"As someone who has worked for the independence of Texas for 20 years, which is guaranteed in Article 1, Section 2 of the Texas Bill of Rights, I consider it a personal attack on everyone who believes in Texas independence to publicly accuse us of a crime and I demand an apology."

No apology was forthcoming. But the resolution passed the convention by a large margin.

Not satisfied with the result, the same delegate introduced a resolution that again leveled the charge of sedition and called for neutering Article 1, Section 2 of the Texas Bill of Rights. After his impassioned and frenetic fear mongering for the resolution, where he directly accused the TNM and its members of sedition, I again responded.

"If this gentleman truly believes that we are guilty of a crime, then a resolution is not the best avenue to deal with this matter. If we are committing a crime, go call 911."

The room erupted in applause and his resolution was massively defeated.

It was proof that fear is a weak weapon and, when someone attempts to use it against a Texan, it will backfire more often than it will work. This is the risk that opponents of Texit seem all too willing to accept and it's why, in the long run, it will fail. Texans do not respond to threats and fear by capitulation. Instead, it is a sure-fire way to get Texans to do exactly the opposite.

A perfect example of how these tactics backfire happened in 2017 in the run-up to the Catalan independence referendum. The Spanish central government chose a strategy of threats and fear to dissuade the people of Catalonia from holding a referendum. They held it anyway. The government chose a strategy of threat, fear, and violence to prevent people from participating in the referendum. People participated anyway. Even as the Spanish batons were crushing Catalan skulls and grandmothers were assaulted at polling locations, the pure joy expressed by the Catalan people in exercising their right of self-determination was transcendent. Even after the vote in favor of independence, the Spanish government found itself faced with the end result of their campaign of fear—more people support independence now than did prior to the referendum. Ana Pousa, who is Spanish by birth but grew up in Catalonia, commented to Fox News that, "They don't realize how many people they converted. Hearing myself saying 'I'm Spanish' sounds strange. Because now it means something different."

Project Fear is exactly that—fear. Fear can be healthy. It can challenge us to avoid dangers that are avoidable. It can cause us to act toward self-preservation to protect our families. But Project Fear is the worst kind of fear. It is an irrational fear whose sole purpose is to cause Texans to act against their best interests. It is used as a tool of oppression, to convince a strong people they are weak, to rob them of a heritage of freedom, and to denigrate them into accepting an inferior position in the world. To paraphrase author Frank Herbert, fear truly is the mind-killer.

Project Fear makes wild assertions, posits impossible scenarios, and allows those who employ its tactics an opportunity to avoid the personal responsibility of being informed and engaging in rational debate. Their incessant questions betray their greatest weakness—their inability to withstand scrutiny and give fact-based, rational answers to legitimate questions.

The influence once held by the Texas version of Project Fear is waning as Texans begin turning the tables. No longer satisfied with smug answers from the opposition, Texit supporters are asking their own questions. The most important question is, "If Texas were already an independent nation, given what I know about the federal government, would I vote to join the union?"

The lack of real answers or legitimate alternatives from Project Fear is proving that they are, as Texans say, "all hat and no cattle."

5 | LAYING THE GROUNDWORK

66The fault, dear Brutus, is not in our stars,
but in ourselves.99

– William Shakespeare, Julius Caesar

One clear lesson is taught for everyone by every single independence movement in recent history. This is especially true for Texas. The fate of any people lies solely in their own hands. Independence and self-government are never given to a passive people. It is never enough to wish for it or dream of it. It requires work, effort, and sacrifice. For most, that effort is limited to casting a vote. For others, it requires much more. In the end, though, the fate of Texit rests singularly in the hands of the people of Texas.

The flip side of this is the reality that, contrary to the droning of some ill-informed pundits, neither the federal government nor any of the other States have a say in the matter. An act of self-government is exclusionary by nature. It takes into account no one and no institutions other than those who are exercising the right. Imagine if another country tried to claim a right to vote in the next U.S. presidential election. The ludicrous notion would be summarily rejected. The same applies here.

While there is no clear point-for-point analog that can be used as a blueprint for Texit, using long-established principles, current law, and generally accepted international norms can help develop a roadmap. Taking the above into account, as well as the practical demands of politics in the 21st century, certain elements absolutely must be present in any process toward independence. Additionally, within that framework, it's important to identify any additional steps or boundaries that will ensure the integrity of, increase participation in, and increase the efficiency of the process.

There are three distinct and separate phases in the Texit process. The question of Texas political status with regard to the Union must first be placed before the people of Texas so they can make their decision. Of necessity, this will be through a referendum. Next, if they choose to Texit, a transitional phase is initiated that will take Texas from membership in the Union to full independence. This includes implementing new structures of governance and implementation of policies that are clearly those of an independent nation-state. It also includes negotiating an orderly exit with the United States government. The final phase sees Texas as a self-governing nation among nations.

Much of the confusion introduced into Texit discussions comes from jumping into debating the later phases of the process and then using objections to potential outcomes in those phases to justify opposing even having a referendum. It is akin to refusing to have children because there is even a small chance that they could do something you didn't like when they got older. These phases must be debated individually and at the proper times. Anything else isn't merely putting the cart before the horse; it's putting a pile of lumber that could potentially be a cart in front of a pregnant horse who hasn't given birth yet to the future cart-puller.

Not that these phases shouldn't be discussed. They should. But they should, at the very least, be discussed and debated separately from one another. However, before engaging in a deep dive on the first phase—a Texit referendum—it is worth taking a look at the lay of the land leading up to a referendum to identify the conditions necessary to start the process.

If getting a referendum was simply a matter of popular opinion, there would have already been one and any discussion of Texit would be confined to reflections on how it looked in the rearview mirror. The more important discussion to have first surrounds this question: with all evidence pointing to enough popular support to make it a foregone conclusion, why hasn't a referendum been held yet or, at the very least, why is it not on the election calendar?

There might be some indication based on the reported numbers of Texit supporters and then using that figure to calculate how many it should take to reasonably expect an independence referendum. For that, you need some method to calculate the tipping point, or the point at which a social or political movement becomes inevitable. Science comes to the rescue. The Social Cognitive Networks Academic Research Center (SCNARC) at Rensselaer Polytechnic Institute released a study in 2011 on the "tipping point" phenomenon that sheds some light on this issue.

Using advanced computational and analytical methods to discover when a minority belief becomes the majority opinion, the scientists at RPI found that, "when just 10 percent of the population holds an unshakable belief, their belief will always be adopted by the majority of the society."

In a release from RPI, they elaborate on the importance of the 10 percent threshold.

"When the number of committed opinion holders is below 10 percent, there is no visible progress in the spread of ideas. It would literally

155

take the amount of time comparable to the age of the universe for this size group to reach the majority," said SCNARC Director Boleslaw Szymanski, the Claire and Roland Schmitt Distinguished Professor at Rensselaer. "Once that number grows above 10 percent, the idea spreads like flame."

By using the standards set forth by RPI and applying those to the number of registered voters in Texas, we can approximate the number of Texit supporters at which getting a Texit referendum becomes a foregone conclusion—between 1,282,593 and 1,510,109. But it's not just any people. According to the study, that number is qualified as "committed opinion holders." This is where things get a bit fuzzy in determining its applicability to Texit.

Because the study used computational and statistical modeling, it was a simple matter to program "unshakeable belief." An unshakable belief is one that is strongly felt and unable to be changed. While this is a simple matter of adjusting an algorithm in computer modeling, it is much harder to define, measure, and predict in a real world scenario with actual people. This challenge probably accounts for the difficulty that social scientists and geopolitical experts have had in using statistical and predictive modeling to predict exactly when these tipping points will occur in mass social and political movements in advance of the occurrence.

An article in the academic journal, the *Journal of Democracy*, titled "China at the Tipping Point? Foreseeing the unForeseeable" articulated this difficulty.

"Regime transitions belong to that paradoxical class of events which are inevitable but not predictable. Other examples are bank runs, currency inflations, strikes, migrations, riots, and revolutions. In retrospect, such events are explainable, even overdetermined. In prospect, however, their timing and character are impossible to anticipate. Such events seem to come closer and closer but do not occur, even when all the conditions are ripe—until suddenly they do."

This is where Texit exists. There is a sense that it's just over the horizon yet, month after month, year after year, people are left wondering why it hasn't happened yet. Texit appears to be well beyond the tipping point that would indicate it is a foregone conclusion. It consistently polls high. In fact, over the last 10 years, those who support Texas leaving the Union have polled equal to or higher than pro-independence Scots, Brits, and Catalans ahead of their respective referenda. All three of these held a referendum, yet Texas has not.

In addition, the depth and diversity of Texans in favor of independence would be the dream of a politician. The support of a majority of Republicans, nearly half of independents, and a substantial percentage of Democrats is enough to get anyone elected in Texas at any level. In short, if Texit were a political candidate, it could get elected to any statewide elected office. Yet still no referendum.

However, those are just polls that ask simple binary questions with no consequence and no mechanism to measure the commitment of the respondent to Texit. And polls, as was shown in the 2016 U.S. presidential election cycle, can be deceiving. To get an idea of how Texit stacks up in the real world, and to get a better sense of the level of commitment of the supporters, one need only compare the leading organizational proponent of Texit, the TNM, to other major political advocacy organizations by measuring their membership or declared support numbers as a percentage of registered voters in the geographic areas they serve.

Among the top ten political organizations considered the most influential across all 50 States, membership figures for the National Organization of Women (0.34 percent), the NAACP (0.21 percent), the National Abortion and Reproductive Rights Action League (0.68 percent), MoveOn (0.21 percent), and LULAC (0.09 percent), represent less than 1 percent of the registered voters. The National Rifle Association (3.42 percent), Americans for Prosperity (1.57 percent) and the U.S. Chamber of Commerce (2.05 percent) are standouts in this group.

Among Texas-focused organizations, the powerful political action committee, Texans For Lawsuit Reform, only represented 0.11 percent of the registered voters in Texas with the current favorite cause of Governor Greg Abbott, the Texas branch of the Convention of States Project, boasting dismal support of only 0.61 percent of Texas voters.

In comparison with all these organizations that are considered mainstream, the TNM has the declared support of 2.31 percent of Texas voters. Even in the seemingly more relevant 21st century political battleground, social media, it has a larger social media following across all platforms than the Texas Republican and Democratic Parties combined.

On the surface, getting a Texit vote should be a slam dunk. After all, the organizations compared above are consistently listed as the most politically powerful and influential pressure groups. They regularly get legislation introduced and enacted. Why does Texit have such a difficult time advancing a referendum?

Taken at face value, Texit should have enough "true believers" to be well past the 10 percent threshold highlighted in the RPI Tipping Point study. The entrance of Texit into the political mainstream, the solid positive polling numbers, and the strength of the support base for its largest advocate organization are all indications of an upward trajectory and momentum. However, while the RPI study predicts the eventual adoption of Texit as the majority opinion, the study does not directly address timescales nor does it take into account real world impediments to achieving the objective.

The fact is that, while Texit may be closer than ever before, an almost undefinable invisible wall seems to be preventing it from achieving "next-level" success. However, if Texit is examined in the perspective of a true binary debate, as a choice with real-world political consequences and only two possible outcomes, as opposed to a basketful of ancillary issues as it is often treated, it becomes easier to identify these impediments and develop a clearer understanding of how they can be overcome.

In looking at Texit from this vantage point, it ceases to be an abstract political theory or a mere thought exercise, and becomes a real and concrete force in a "war of ideas," with one side being "leave" and the other side "remain." In fact, this is the only honest way to evaluate Texit since it is exactly how the question will be put to voters in an actual referendum. When the people of Texas actually get to vote on the issue, the choice will be solely between "leave" or "remain." Simplifying it this way allows us to categorize every actor as being on one side or the other and allows the objective evaluation of every action as to its benefit or detriment to its particular side. It also brings crystal clarity to the real impediments slowing the advance of the Texit cause.

The explanation for these challenges in the war of ideas may lie in the work of Carl von Clausewitz, the early 19th century Prussian military theorist, whose *On War* has been used as a primer into the conduct of warfare. Its use over time has expanded beyond the traditional battlefield and found a new home in explaining challenges in the political and business arenas. In fact, the *Warfighting* manual of the United States Marine Corps directly quotes Clausewitz on the difficulties faced when two opposing viewpoints contend for dominance.

"Portrayed as a clash between two opposing wills, war appears a simple enterprise. In practice, the conduct of war becomes extremely difficult because of the countless factors that impinge on it. These factors collectively have been called friction, which Clausewitz described as 'the force that makes the apparently easy so difficult.' Friction is the force that resists all action and saps energy. It makes the simple difficult and the difficult seemingly impossible."

While friction plays a significant role in traditional warfare, the role is significantly greater when dealing with social and political movements. Armies are rigid in structure and discipline, with in-built mechanisms to lessen friction. In short, there are far fewer variables in the equation. Mass social and political movements, on the other hand, often exhibit less discipline and suffer from internal contests over messaging, lack of experience, and conflicting personalities that can exponentially amplify any friction.

While there is a tendency to focus on the external opposition to Texit, the actual challenges to achieving Texit are primarily internal and, when taken as a whole, are the reason that Texit is at the threshold but can't seem to get in the door. To this point, if you examine the tactics used by those who oppose Texit, they are not direct assaults on the fundamental tenets of Texit supporters. They are, under the surface, attempting to bully, undermine, weaken, and demoralize the belief of Texit supporters and beat them into unthinking submission. To a large degree, they have been successful.

Their success weakens the foundation of support and, consequently, magnifies all the other challenges. These challenges are systemic to the point of being nearly impossible to unravel so they can be addressed individually. The key word, though, is "nearly." There are a handful of readily identifiable impediments to pushing Texit beyond the tipping point. While these impediments do not affect every supporter of Texit, the presence of one or more of these in significant percentages of Texit supporters helps explain why Texit is at the door but hasn't crossed the threshold.

ATOMIZATION

A solid example of the challenge this poses is the effect of the constant refrain from the media and half-baked academics claiming that a very small minority of Texans support Texas leaving the Union. There is an unrelenting stream of loud, pro-federal propaganda that casts Texit supporters as political outliers. The sting of being labeled "un-American" is often enough to shove many Texit supporters back in their holes. If the media dismisses or outright ignores the strength of Texit support or, when it bothers to cover the issue, heaps on ridicule, then it serves to atomize the supporters.

No matter the strength of the poll numbers in favor of Texit, supporters still feel like they are an insignificant minority. This causes supporters to enter into a self-imposed exile and hide from one another, never knowing their true numbers and always underestimating their true power. In short, they have been shouted and ridiculed into silence by the actual minority's opinion.

Gene Sharp, the author of *From Dictatorship To Democracy* labels this phenomenon atomization. In short, if a regime and its cronies can increase the perceived barriers between people and groups of people and convince people they are alone or are an insignificant minority in their opposition to the regime, they become effectively neutralized. There is no need to create martyrs if you simply make people feel alone in their beliefs.

Right now, Texit supporters are highly atomized, falling prey to the greatest weapon in the arsenal of the opposition—the belief that few share this opinion. In the previously cited RPI study, the effect of this was clear.

"In general, people do not like to have an unpopular opinion and are always seeking to try locally to come to consensus. We set up this dynamic in each of our models," said SCNARC research associate and corresponding paper author Sameet Sreenivasan. "To accomplish this, each of the individuals in the models 'talked' to each other about their opinion. If the listener held the same opinions as the speaker, it reinforced the listener's belief. If the opinion was different, the listener considered it and moved on to talk to another person. If that person also held this new belief, the listener then adopted that belief. As agents of change start to convince more and more people, the situation begins to change," Sreenivasan said. "People begin to question their own views at first and then completely adopt the new view to spread it even further. If the true believers just influenced their neighbors, that wouldn't change anything within the larger system, as we saw with percentages less than 10."

Regardless of how effective this tactic has been in the past, recent political successes and high profile activism from leading proponents of Texit are increasing the resistance of supporters to this angle of attack. The recent public show of widespread support at the Republican State Convention, coupled with political candidates being forced to publicly declare their support for an independence referendum, has helped. But, until Texit supporters begin to actively connect with other supporters of Texit, it will continue to be an issue.

POLITICAL APATHY

The natural byproduct of atomization is hopelessness, which leads to political apathy. Often all it takes to neutralize a Texit supporter is a declaration from a friend, family member, or someone with perceived authority that "it will never happen." In the minds of many Texit supporters, if Texit will never happen, then there is no chance for self-government. If there is no chance to reclaim the right of self-government, then elections specifically, and the entire political system in general, simply do not matter.

It is this sort of political apathy that prevents Texit supporters from realizing their full political potential and affecting the outcome of elections. If Texit supporters don't flex their electoral muscle, the political apathy on the issue is represented in the one place where a referendum must first receive majority support—the Texas Legislature.

In 2011, Texans came within hours of having a piece of legislation filed that would have given them a vote on independence. State Representative Leo Berman, a former lieutenant colonel in the United States Army, had agreed to file a bill drafted by the TNM that would have placed the question of Texas independence on the ballot in November of that year.

During his tenure in the Texas House, Berman had gained a reputation as a "straight shooter" and had become a vocal proponent for State-level action to combat illegal immigration. Frustrated with the lack of action on bills he filed in the previous session dealing with the issue of illegal immigration, he laid the responsibility squarely at the feet of Texas Speaker of the House Joe Straus.

Berman's frustration with Straus' leadership led Berman to file to run for Speaker in the 2011 session. It was a battle that he ultimately lost and the results of that loss would have a direct bearing on Texit.

After agreeing to file the independence referendum legislation, Berman received a phone call summoning him to Straus' office. Fifteen minutes later, Berman withdrew his support. He would later confide that Straus had issued him an ultimatum. "If you file the independence bill, none of your immigration bills will see the light of day in this session."

Berman made a pragmatic decision and deferred to Straus. However, even after withdrawing his support for the independence referendum bill, none of Berman's bills dealing with illegal immigration passed the Texas House anyway.

Were Texit supporters politically engaged at a sufficient level in 2011, this scenario would have played out much differently than it did. Straus would likely not have been Speaker of the House and the Texas Legislature would have been populated by a majority of pro-independence elected representatives who would have had Berman's back.

However, moving forward, this situation is likely to change. Emboldened by their newfound connections to the larger community of Texit supporters, they are starting to do the math and are realizing that there are enough of them in every area of the State to effect the outcome of nearly any State-level election if, and only if, they vote as a bloc. But it only matters if they make Texit a reason to vote for or against a candidate and stick to their guns. In short, Texit supporters have to be willing to eschew the normal political divisions and partisan politics to make it their one and only voting issue.

POLITICAL AMATEURISM

Even if Texit supporters overcome the atomization and form a political community, the next challenge is, perhaps, more daunting. It's not enough to *have* potential political power. It must be wielded like a weapon and used effectively.

Texit supporters who have overcome the imposed silence and engage in the political process are some of the most vocal proponents— up to a certain point. It's not enough to know or believe. Independence takes work. This is where Texit supporters are most challenged. Being vocal is not enough to get the job done. "SECEDE" bumper stickers are great and there are plenty on the roads, but mere bumper sticker activism won't win the day for Texit. Social media is a great tool, but a "LIKE" on Facebook or a sporadic tweet is no replacement for good ol' on-the-ground political activism.

Texit supporters fall woefully short when compared to the level of activism shown by those who advocate for policies that centralize more power in Washington, D.C. The simple fact is that the federal apologists outwork Texit supporters at a staggering level in the traditional methods of political outreach. For every door knocked on or phone called by a Texit supporter, there are thousands made by the other side.

I am convinced, however, that this is not due to a lack of belief. Rather, it is a result of the vast majority of Texit supporters being political neophytes. Because of long-term political apathy, most have never participated in organized political outreach at the level required to move an issue like Texit forward at a substantial pace. Therefore, many reside in a comfort zone that limits their activism to bumper stickers, t-shirts, and social media. It's far easier to click a button on a screen than it is to knock on a stranger's door. While these outreach methods have some value in spreading the message, they cannot exist as the sole or even the primary means of political engagement.

To put it in Texan terms, when Sam Houston commanded the Texian Army, he won the Battle of San Jacinto with a ragtag army of amateur volunteer soldiers, but they knew, at a minimum, how to fight at a basic level that was equivalent to the Mexican Army. While the volunteers enlisted as amateurs, by the time the guns fell silent at San Jacinto, they were battle-hardened professional soldiers. They did what was personally required of them to prepare to fight and to win.

Increasing the numbers of politically savvy and engaged Texit supporters is an absolute requirement to get a referendum on the issue. Notwithstanding the critics who insist that Texit requires consent of the other States or those voices who advocate for extra-legal paths to independence, the true gatekeeper on the Texit referendum is the Texas Legislature. Because a referendum on the issue requires legislation, it will require either a constitutional amendment, not requiring the governor's signature, or a simple bill with support from the governor. Either way, majority support of both houses of the Texas Legislature is not optional. It is a solid requirement. That majority is only achieved by effectively wielding political power at a sufficient level of professionalism to get the job done.

This is a similar challenge to the one faced by the U.K. Independence Party, which famously pressured the U.K. government into calling for a Brexit referendum. From its inception until 2014, the consensus was that UKIP posed no significant electoral threat to the existing power structure in the U.K. In the minds of pundits, UKIP's existence was nothing more than a hobby of its narcissist-in-chief, Nigel Farage. Even when UKIP achieved major victories in the 2014 European Parliament elections, the success was viewed as an aberration and it was predicted that UKIP would fold like Superman on laundry day over the following summer and would not be a factor in the 2015 general election. In the words of Matthew Goodwin, reporting for *The Telegraph*, "There is a sense that it remains an amateur party and on the campaign trail looks more like Dad's Army than a ruthlessly organised insurgency."

Even into the Newark by-election in June of 2014, it seemed that the pundits were being proven right. In sharp contrast to other major U.K. political parties, in the Newark campaign UKIP did not possess sufficient manpower, either through paid staff or volunteers and, therefore, was not nearly active enough to get its message across or mobilize its supporters at a time when it was most critical. The result, according to Goodwin, was that "voters experienced less contact with UKIP than with the main parties." In short, potential voters saw much less of UKIP, receiving fewer leaflets, seeing even fewer billboards, and missing much-needed interaction with UKIP activists and volunteers.

This lack of staff and volunteers meant that systems that are common to nearly all successful campaigns were virtually absent in the UKIP campaigns. UKIP did not have, or could not fully implement, a basic system for identifying voters. Goodwin noted that, "As the main parties employed sophisticated computer software, Ukippers merely scrawled their notes on pages of A4 and often collected the wrong information."

In addition, there were other serious amateur mistakes. The campaign vigorously implemented an "every door policy" for the explicit purpose of finding voters who had fallen off the rolls. Instead, the effect was to mobilize their opposition. Additionally, activists and volunteers, who were readily identified as belonging to the party, would often go on embarrassing social media tirades with little or no discipline meted out for the damage caused to the party and its message.

The effect was to be expected. In Newark and other locations, UKIP was obliterated at the polls. In this instance, political amateurism had a real, definable cost. The leadership of UKIP did the best they could with what they had, but leadership in political parties and movements can only create and implement systems. It takes the supporters upping their games to make it work.

UKIP was able to recognize this fact and make significant changes, which led to UKIP becoming the third largest party in the U.K. in the 2015 general election. They honed their larger message and implemented a new professional voter identification system that enabled them to connect with local voters in a way they hadn't been able to before. They developed a better system for recruiting and training volunteers and demanded that they be professional in their dealings with one another and the public, exchanging street clothes and casual attire for business and professional attire. They even implemented new rules for how members represent the party online and in social media, instituting formal disciplinary action procedures for those who crossed the line. Goodwin reflected on the change. "While it is tempting to dismiss UKIP as a band of amateur populists, the reality is that it is no longer an amateur operation."

Like it or not, all electorates, including potential supporters of Texit, have expectations of how political movements should look, act, and speak. While it is fun to romanticize about a day and age where it is only the core message that matters, the fact is that this is not that day and age. For Texit to have that breakthrough moment, its supporters are going to have to come to the realization that the expectation of professionalism from their fellow Texans regarding political activism must be, at a minimum, met and very likely exceeded.

SHORT-TERM THINKING AND
THE CREDIBILITY GAP

The challenge with political apathy or amateurism is that those who fall into either category generally maintain some superficial awareness and engagement in the political process. Those who still vote largely restrict their activities to the voting booth. The effect is that those who superficially participate become trained to think in short two- to four-year cycles. Much like research that has shown that the maximum attention span of the TV generation became synchronized with the duration of programming between commercial breaks, many of those who are superficially engaged in the political process have had their cycles of commitment synchronized to the election cycles.

In their minds, if something isn't achieved within the timeframe of one or two election cycles, then it is a total failure and is completely dead. Often they look at the first defeat or setback as fatal. And it is, at least where their support is concerned. However, those who are most connected to a political community and who are politically engaged, seem immune. Because of this, a sizable number of Texit supporters, through this conditioning and as a byproduct of their atomization and prolonged political apathy, contend with this challenge.

Some point to a lack of major success in advancing Texit as the real issue. Yet one can look at some of the aforementioned examples of modern independence movements and see how this short-term thinking is really a failure in personal mindset and perspective. Scotland sought independence for 800 years. The Scottish National Party was formed in 1934 and the party didn't win its first seat in Parliament until 1945. It didn't win an electoral mandate until 2007. It followed with an independence referendum seven years later. The U.K. Independence Party started pushing for a Brexit referendum in 1993 with the Labour

Party first pushing for the same referendum in 1974. It was finally held in 2016. The modern political movement for the independence of Catalonia traces its roots back to 1922, yet it wouldn't see a formal referendum on the issue until 2017.

In sharp contrast, the modern movement for Texas independence can trace its roots back to 1996, with the TNM not seeing the light of day until 2005. The TNM's first legislative and political successes didn't even start until eight years later. In comparison to these recently successful examples from around the world, the modern movement for Texit is in its infancy.

Much like the other impediments, this type of short-term think-ing has real world consequences on advancing Texit. Lacking proper perspective, Texit supporters plagued by short-term thinking are prone to discouragement. This discouragement leads to one of two distinct actions. Either the discouraged fall prey to those who promise a short-cut or they return to their previous status as politically inert.

Many well-intentioned supporters fall victim to the purveyors of the "quicker, faster, better" sales pitch. Texans want their grievances with the federal government addressed as quickly as possible. Those that identify Texit as the best solution want Texas independence to hap-pen sooner rather than later. After all, if there is a way that it can be done faster and better, anyone would be a fool to ignore the possibil-ity. However, if you couple this with political amateurism, it becomes too common for pied pipers to lead Texit supporters into deeper discouragement.

This has not gone unnoticed by the political class, which is quick to use it to their advantage for short-term political gain. Rick Perry, after playing coy with the issue of Texit in 2009, utterly failed to protect Texas from federal overreach as the governor of Texas. Instead of using his position to champion a vote on Texit, he wrote a book and is now a member of Trump's cabinet as the head of a federal department he loudly declared should be abolished.

Greg Abbott seems destined to follow in Perry's footsteps. As attorney general, Abbott's strategy in battling federal overreach could be condensed to "Tweet, Sue, Lose, Repeat." As attorney general, he scuttled talks between then-Lt. Governor David Dewhurst, representatives from the TNM, and his office because his primary concern was his impending campaign for governor and his fear of how it would look. Now that he is governor, he no longer has the power to sue the federal government, thereby streamlining his strategy to "Tweet & Repeat." However, he did take a note from Perry's book, now using the phrase of "If Texas was its own country..." to elicit applause.

Even as these two high-profile politicians publicly pandered to Texit supporters and privately derailed their efforts, there were many who vested all their hopes for a quick Texit into these two men and were let down. These two are just some of the high-profile examples. Over the years, Texit supporters have been pitched every form of quick fix for the Union or faster path to independence. Whether it's the latest political messiah running for federal office who is promising, "This time will be different" to the newest political fads like "Get Out Of Our House" or Convention of the States, they have all been more hype than hope and are doomed to failure.

The growth of social media has amplified this phenomenon, especially when it comes to Texit. Anyone with 15 minutes and minimal computer skills can set up a page or group on social media, cobble together 15 or 20 followers, and declare themselves the "Voice of Texas Independence," thereby creating additional noise that those who are seeking real answers and solutions related to Texit find increasingly harder to sift through. The damage to the cause of Texit cannot be overstated. In the era where social media makes it difficult to tell real news from news generated by a Russian troll farm, the hit to credibility can be, and often is, massive and worldwide in a matter of minutes.

Occasionally, some of these online actors attempt to make the jump into the real world. Declaring themselves an organization or running for office under the independence banner, things take a turn from annoyance to farce. Some of these organizations actually make an attempt to appear credible. One such organization floated some of the most ridiculous ideas ever presented in an attempt to address serious concerns that Texans have with Texit. Promoted as "plans," these ideas more closely resembled below-average junior high civics projects than well thought-out policy positions. For example, one such plank of their allegedly well thought-out and well-researched plan proposed transferring desalinated water from the Gulf of Mexico through oil pipelines back to West Texas, declaring that it was perfectly feasible and safe because "oil and water don't mix."

Another small collection of malcontents, who are best known for getting arrested for pretending to be government officials and ostensibly advocates for an independent Texas, recently made a very negative statement about the Catholic faith. Congratulations, guys. You just alienated approximately 20 percent of Texans directly and over half of Texans who consider themselves religious indirectly. Not only that, you tied it directly to the cause of Texas independence.

The point is not to ridicule these folks. It is to highlight the fact that, even with the damage they cause and their obvious inability to ever get Texas out of a failing Union, some people, beset by short-term thinking, view them as a viable alternative to the mainstream Texit movement. In doing so, they represent a disruptive and fragmenting force that creates serious credibility issues for Texit among those who are undecided, even causing some that were for independence to throw their hands up in disgust and give up on the idea entirely.

Getting and maintaining credibility is extremely important for Texit to advance. For every action that robs it of credibility, it takes a dozen more to regain it. The effect of losing credibility plays out predictably. When credibility becomes shaky, people who would otherwise be inclined to support Texit or, at a minimum, entertain the notion, lose hope that it can be done. This affects the number of true believers, which affects the amount of money people put into Texit. With no money, it becomes impossible to become a serious player at the ballot box, which is reflected in a Texit-averse Legislature. A Texit-averse Legislature means a leadership in the Legislature that will stop at nothing to prevent Texans from having a referendum on this issue. This leads to frustrated pro-Texit supporters, who then fall prey to the pied pipers who promise a way to do it "quicker and better." So the cycle goes.

For Texit to advance in a timely manner, Texit supporters will have to adopt a more long-term, forward-thinking, disciplined, and discerning approach.

DUAL IDENTITIES

I am often invited to speak at meetings of civic and political organizations throughout Texas. These meetings are generally very patriotic affairs. Invariably, attendees are asked to stand facing the flag of the United States, place their hands over their hearts and recite these words:

"I pledge allegiance to the flag of the United States of America, and to the republic for which it stands, one nation under God, indivisible, with liberty and justice for all."

Then the attendees are directed to face the Texas flag and recite the Texas Pledge.

"Honor the Texas flag; I pledge allegiance to thee, Texas, one state under God, one and indivisible."

The Texas Pledge is sometimes conducted as a normal part of the meeting agenda. Other times I'm fairly certain they tack it on because I am there. Either way, the situation always strikes me as funny.

Here is a group of people who are the most patriotic of the patriotic, who often despise socialism in all of its forms, first pledging their allegiance to the flag of a union and declaring its indivisibility, not realizing that the words were penned by an avowed socialist. Then they turn and pledge their allegiance to Texas shortly before introducing the guy who is going to spend the next 30 to 45 minutes explaining that it's not possible to hold dual allegiances to equivalent political bodies and that whole indivisible thing in the U.S. pledge is really a myth.

It's also fairly typical for me to conduct a question-and-answer section after my remarks. There is almost always that one person who takes the floor to express how he or she believes that Texit is the "way to go" while decked head to toe in American flag gear. Less common are the people who begin their questioning by declaring their love for Texas and their opposition to Texit, following it with a pledge of undying love and support for the federal system they previously agreed is beyond repair.

I chuckle, but I never point out the irony of the situation. There is no need. I'm certain that, either immediately after or at some time down the road, they will reflect on that moment and it will hit them like it did me. This is not isolated to those who are undecided about Texit, either. Through contacts with thousands of Texas voters, it has not gone unnoticed that some of the quickest to pledge their support to Texit are ones decked out in the most American flag clothing. It could be, and has been, argued that these folks are deeply committed to American principles and, because of how far the rest of the Union has strayed from those principles, now support Texas leaving the Union to preserve those principles. However, the mere act of clinging to the symbols and identity of the United States is another significant impediment to the advance of Texit.

Looking back at the first Texas Revolution and the American Revolution, I find no examples of anyone who played a significant role in either who claimed that it was possible to maintain an allegiance to the body from which they were separating while declaring their allegiance to the cause of birthing a new nation among nations. In fact, every contemporaneous source indicates the exact opposite.

In Thomas Jefferson's "Declaration of the Causes and Necessity for Taking Up Arms," he emphatically states that, "Our attachment to no nation on earth should supplant our attachment to liberty," thereby discouraging continued allegiance to nations or institutions that are detrimental to liberty. In the previously cited Letter From The Committee of Safety of Liberty in 1835, its authors were clear that there was no middle ground.

"The contest is for liberty or slavery; for life or death; for the tranquil possession of the country we have redeemed from barbarism, or a forcible ejectment from it. It admits of no neutrals."

Both declarations of independence are clear in their call for an "eternal political separation," but it's safe to assume that the separation in spirit and mind happened well before the words were committed to paper. I cannot find any examples of those who fought in the American Revolution continuing to refer to themselves as British nor are there any accounts from soldiers at the Alamo or in Houston's army referring to themselves as Mexicans.

Lest we think of these as artifacts from a distant age, a quick glance at modern movements for self-determination says otherwise. In Scotland's push for independence, there was not a Union Jack flag among those advocating for their exit from the U.K. If you asked pro-independence Scots whether they were Scottish or British, you'd likely get a quizzical look before an emphatic declaration of "I'm Scottish!" During the campaign for Brexit, the "Leave" campaigners never displayed the flag of the European Union alongside the Union Jack. In fact, the presence of the European flag on British soil was seen as an affront and a direct attack on the Britishness of the U.K. You would be hard pressed to find a single person who voted "Leave" that considered him or herself both British and European. They would readily admit that Britain was part of Europe by virtue of geography, but that's where it ended.

However, this mindset is on full display every September 11th in Barcelona, when 1.5 million Catalans take to the streets to celebrate a famous battle in their history, celebrate their national identity, and express their desire for independence. The streets are a sea of Senyera estelada, Catalonia's version of the Lone Star flag. What is nowhere in evidence is the flag of Spain.

For self-determination movements to make significant progress, they must identify as something different than that which they are leaving. If there is no distinction, then there is really no reason to leave. That's why Catalans identify as Catalans, Brexiteers identify as Brits, and Scots identify as Scots. It is also why, for Texit to have that breakthrough moment, Texit advocates must begin to transition their thinking to identify as Texans and Texans only.

In reality, if the United States was the federative republic it was intended to be, this is how Texans and the people of other States would already think. The fact that this is actually an issue is further proof that the Union has mutated beyond its purpose. The federal system was never meant by its Founders to subsume the individual identity and character of its constituent States or the people within them.

One could reasonably argue that this has been perhaps the biggest impediment to pushing past the tipping point. It causes even the most ardent Texit supporters to have an inconsistent worldview and to take seemingly contradictory positions on issues of the day. It creates a lack of cohesion leading to a "hokey-pokey" mentality, where one day they find their right foot in Texit and the next day with their right foot out.

MONEY

In 2017, one Texas state representative confessed to me what he personally saw as the major impediment to getting Texas independence referendum legislation filed in the Legislature.

"If I file this bill, the 'Establishment' will absolutely recruit a challenger to run against me in the primaries. I will likely have to spend over $250,000 to defend my seat and get a few thousand more people in my district out to the polls."

In short, he knew that political battles take resources and that Texit was resource-poor.

Even with all of the public success of the TNM, a recent report highlights the challenge faced by a lack of money. The 2016 annual report from the organization showed that the organization operates on an annual budget of $42,000 per year, forcing them to rely exclusively on volunteers for all top-level positions, lean on personal contributions from those same volunteers, and focus exclusively on social media, earned media, and on-the-ground outreach from a handful of active volunteers to get the word out.

Yet, in Texas, much like other places, the cost of political campaigns is higher than it's ever been. The amount of money needed to consistently and effectively reach voters is staggering. A *Texas Tribune* report from 2017 examined the campaign finance reports from the 2016 general election. Its findings put a concrete figure on the problem.

"In the most closely watched Texas race last year—U.S. Rep. Will Hurd's re-election bid against former U.S. Rep. Pete Gallego—Hurd won by fewer than 3,000 votes. But Hurd, a Republican, spent big for that win, shelling out $29.12 per vote, among the highest in the state. Gallego, a Democrat, spent $15.75 per vote."

In Greg Abbott's campaign for governor in 2014, he spent in excess of $8 million dollars and received a little over 1.2 million votes, an average of $6.65 per vote. These figures are typical in the modern political system. If candidates or causes want even a chance to win, they have to be prepared to shell out the money to reach voters.

When these figures are applied to Texit, the challenge is readily identifiable. To connect with and organize the number of people necessary for Texit to hit the tipping point, it will take a minimum spend of $8 to $10 million. That's just to get to the starting line. When the math is applied to actually campaigning in a Texit referendum, the buy-in starts at $50 million.

On the surface, it seems like Texit has a money problem. It doesn't. A survey commissioned by the TNM gives a snapshot of the financial demographics of Texit supporters. Some 49 percent earn between $50,000 to $100,000 per year and another 25 percent earn more. A full 4 percent earn more than $500,000 a year. These numbers show that Texit supporters possess the resources required to significantly impact its progress.

In reality, Texit has a donor problem. If every currently declared supporter of Texit contributed $27 tomorrow, the initial $10 million target would be achieved. That, however, is with 100 percent participation, which is completely unrealistic given what is known about how few people, not just Texit supporters, actually give political contributions.

A report from the Center for Responsive Politics analyzed campaign finance data from the 2015-2016 federal elections and found that an extremely small percentage of people across the States actually financially participated in the political process. A scant 0.52 percent of the U.S. population gave in excess of $200 in campaign contributions, with only 0.08 percent giving more than $2,700.

Taken alone, these percentages seem paltry, but they add up. In that same election cycle, the total given by those giving less than $2,700 was right at $1 billion. The contributions over $2,700 totaled in excess of $3.5 billion. Contributions of less than $200 amounted for a staggering $1.5 billion. During the height of the presidential campaign cycle in 2016, Trump's campaign reported that, in the month of July, his campaign raised $35.8 million from 517,000 small donors each giving an average of $69 each. According to the *Washington Post*, "(Hillary) Clinton supporters contributed $8.7 million between 8 p.m. on July 28, the night Clinton addressed the Democratic National Convention in Philadelphia, and 8 p.m. the next day." In a 24-hour period, Clinton raised more money than Abbott spent for his entire 2014 gubernatorial campaign.

Raising the money to move the needle on Texit is possible. However, the other impediments to Texit create the donor issue and leave the movement cash-starved. The fragmented, politically apathetic don't want to donate because they have no hope that Texit will actually happen. The politically naïve deny the reality of the role that money plays in the process. The myopic and double-minded shuffle their financial support from one cause to the other, lining the pockets of snake-oil salesmen who don't possess the ability or the desire to deliver on Texit. This lack of cash restricts the momentum of Texit and leaves its proponents fighting like guerillas rather than the well-oiled political machine that is required.

BRINGING IT TOGETHER

However daunting these challenges seem, they aren't insurmountable. Virtually every other modern movement for independence has faced the same challenges. While each had differences rooted in their own culture, political system, and circumstances, they were all variations on the same themes.

The political class would love nothing more than to see Texit stuck at the point of seeming inevitability. For the opposition, it would display an ever-present boogeyman they could use to mobilize their supporters without ever having to directly address the uncomfortable issues raised by an actual debate on Texit. Pandering politicians would have a ready-made pool of passionate Texans who could flirt with the idea to maintain support for their campaigns or parties, filling their campaign coffers, without ever giving Texit supporters what they really want.

Bad news for them: Nothing stays the same forever.

Texit supporters, slowly but surely, are beginning to recognize the value of networking with one another. They are beginning to understand that exercising the right of self-government doesn't have to wait until a Texit referendum and are learning the skills necessary to effectively compete in the political process. For many, this has been like transforming from a goldfish, waiting at the surface of the water to be fed, into a shark that is singularly fixed on its prey. Make no mistake; those who have made this transformation have smelled blood in the political waters. This has led to a broadening of their vision and a recommitment to seeing Texit through to the end. This broader vision has led to a general intolerance for the peddlers of false hope and a new discerning eye that sees the role of the Texit supporter transformed from passive cheerleader to the immune system for the cause acting to protect it at all costs.

While there has been movement on some of these issues that should be encouraging to supporters of Texit, the issues of double-mindedness in relation to the Union and the general failure to accept the role money plays in the political process requires serious attention for Texit to move to the next level. However, the momentum on solving the other issues is likely to create movement on these as well.

The real difficulty comes in determining when Texit will eventually "toe up" to the starting line. Frankly, there is no way to know. Outside of some major external catalyzing event affecting the majority of Texans, it will take smaller, more personalized catalyzing moments to strengthen the individual political will of Texit supporters and challenge their character in such a way that there is no option for them other than forward to Texit.

Given the trajectory of Texit, lessons learned from other modern independence movements, with an understanding of the "field of play" and the current level of friction within the movement, Texit is on the cusp of becoming an inevitable and unstoppable force. As these impediments continue to resolve, it's time to buckle up because a Texit referendum is coming.

6 | THE TEXAS INDEPENDENCE REFERENDUM

> ❝All political power is inherent in the people, and all free governments are founded on their authority, and instituted for their benefit. The faith of the people of Texas stands pledged to the preservation of a republican form of government, and, subject to this limitation only, they have at all times the inalienable right to alter, reform or abolish their government in such manner as they may think expedient. ❞
>
> *– Texas Constitution, Article 1, Section 2*

The first real step in Texit is the one that seems to get the most attention. I once heard a political consultant refer to it as the "sexiest" part of the process. Here it is in a nutshell: Texans vote on it. While that may seem like an oversimplification, it's not. The entire issue will literally come down to a question, two choices, and the decision made by the people of Texas. In reality, it's not the vote that's exciting; instead, it's what comes before and after the vote.

There is one fundamental and immutable truth about the Texit process. Where there is a legal path to Texit, it must be followed. There are no secret processes or hidden clauses in the old documents that can be used. There are no shortcuts. It boils down to what laws and processes are on the books right now and how they can be applied to resolving the issue of Texas independence. That means it absolutely, at a minimum, must culminate in a free and fair vote of the people of Texas—a referendum.

Although Texas v. White as a Supreme Court decision is a total mess, it does highlight the importance of putting the question to a vote of the people and the importance placed on the process that Texas, or any State, undertakes to extract itself from the Union and assert its independence.

In that ruling, Chief Justice Chase made specific mention of the fact that the process Texas used to leave the Union in 1861 was irregular. Indeed, it was extremely irregular. It was those irregularities that he used as a pretense to jump to some ludicrous conclusions. Caught up in the "secession fever" sweeping over the States, there were calls from prominent Texans of the time for Texas to follow suit. Sam Houston, the governor of Texas, still hopeful that there was a political solution that could hold the Union together, refused to call the Texas Legislature into a special session to take up the secession question. Led by Texas Supreme Court Chief Justice Oran M. Roberts, an effort was launched to bypass Houston's resistance and directly elect delegates for a secession convention.

On January 8, 1861, elections were held for delegates all throughout Texas. However, the election was fraught with irregularities. In many areas, the vote was not carried out by ballot. Instead, it was conducted in a public meeting with the results being tallied by a show of hands or a voice vote. In an attempt to bring order back into the process, Houston finally called for a special session of the legislature in January of 1861 in hopes that the legislators would reject the usurpation of their elected authority and declare the convention illegal. He was wrong. The legislators placed their seal of approval on the convention and turned the secession question over to the delegates.

The delegates drafted and passed Articles of Secession. Houston, however, still felt it his duty as a statesman to bring some order to the process. Although he was opposed to Texas moving to leave the Union and joining the newly formed Confederacy, he believed in a principle he had fought for in the Texas Revolution. That principle was enshrined in the Texas Bill of Rights in the Republic of Texas Constitution of 1836, was included in the State of Texas Constitution of 1845, and exists in our current state constitution. In 1836, the principle was enshrined using these words:

"All political power is inherent in the People, and all free governments are founded on their authority, and instituted for their benefit; and they have at all times an inalienable right to alter their government in such manner as they may think proper."

Houston, perhaps recalling the men at the Alamo who had died for this principle, declared that the only way he would recognize the decision for Texas to leave the Union was for the question to be put to a vote of the people. In his mind, Texas had entered the Union by consent of the people and, therefore, the people must signal a clear indication that they wanted to leave. In a referendum held on February 23, 1861, by a vote of 44,317 to 13,020, Texans sent their message.

Yet, from the standpoint of process, the referendum was the only silver lining. The cloud over the legitimacy of the process in 1860-1861 highlights why, when it comes to independence, you cannot sacrifice process and the rule of law for expediency, especially if you want to ensure that the result is uncontested.

Since the right of any State to leave the Union is implied and, therefore, rests solely with the States, the process to extract a State from the Union is not specifically defined. In short, there is no manual for an exit from the United States. Where the United Kingdom had Article 50 in the Treaty of Lisbon that laid out a basic framework for Brexit, in the instance of States leaving the United States, there is nothing similar. In fact, the generation that founded the United States believed that, if a State chose to leave the Union, how it did so was completely up to the

State that was leaving, as long as it followed the norms of a republican form of government. In essence, there could be 50 completely different processes, all with the same result.

Lest we think this is somehow unusual, it is important to note that, as self-determination has spread around the world over the past century, the processes undertaken to achieve independence have been less than consistent. However, this lack of consistency should not be taken as a signal of insurmountable difficulty or impossibility for a people seeking the right of self-government. These differences in process stem from the natural differences that exist between nations and states in governmental structure, culture, law, and history, not from a fundamental flaw in the principle of self-determination. It does make it difficult to utilize any single example as a step-by-step manual for any other nation, state, or people.

Even without perfect clarity, the process under which independence is achieved has been vitally important in the last 100 years for one reason—recognition. Recognition of acts of self-determination has generally come down to whether a new nation-state's independence is recognized by the international community that has recognized the new nation-state, and to what degree recognition occurred. But there are two other layers that have not received a fair examination and are fundamental parts of the process.

The first of these is internal recognition. In short, the people of Texas themselves must accept the process as democratic, consistent with existing law, and congruent with their understanding of the principles of self-government. If the people don't recognize the process, they won't respect the results of the process.

Also important, but for completely different reasons, is recognition of the legitimacy of the process by the United States. The reason we should, at least partially, be concerned about the United States' reaction to the process is practical. Amicable separations are far better than contentious ones. It is obviously desirable to have friendly relations with the United States. As it is our closest neighbor, along with Mexico, we will have issues of trade, travel, defense, and many others that will benefit from cooperation that is only possible if contentious issues are kept to a minimum. That only happens in the absence of a cloud of illegitimacy hanging over the process.

One certain way to sabotage the potential for good relations is to give the United States any opportunity to cast doubt on the process used to gain independence. The entire process, in the eyes of the United States, will rise or fall, not on Texas v. White, but on these words in Article IV, Section 4 of the United States Constitution:

"The United States shall guarantee to every state in this union, a republican form of government..."

It was this section that was used as a cornerstone argument to retroactively justify the use of military force against the seceding States in the 1860s. While it is far-fetched to think that Texit might spark the use of military force in the 21st century, the use of a process that did not follow generally accepted principles of a "republican form of government" would be more than enough for the United States to reject the results and, at a minimum, refuse to recognize a decision to Texit.

The good news is that the same process that satisfies the requirements for internal recognition is also consistent with the generally accepted principles of a republican form of government. The better news is that the United States has a decades-long track record on the issue of self-determination that would make any objection to a legitimate process wholly inconsistent with decades of well-established foreign policy and would destroy any credibility they would have on the issue for generations.

For instance, take one of the most controversial decisions on self-determination ever taken by the United States. In 2008, Kosovo, a fully integrated region of Serbia with a population of approximately 2 million, unilaterally declared independence from its mother country. Over the objections of Serbia and the majority of the international community, the United States was one of the first countries to recognize Kosovo as an independent nation-state.

In the years leading up to the declaration, the champion of Kosovar independence was none other than President George W. Bush. In 2007, Bush lobbied hard on the international stage for a negotiated independence for Kosovo. Speaking during a state visit to Albania, Bush signaled U.S. solidarity declaring, "Independence is the goal. That's what the people of Kosovo need to know."

When negotiations between Kosovo and Serbia broke down, the Assembly of Kosovo drafted and ratified a declaration of independence. This prompted immediate recognition by the United States, with Bush declaring it would "bring peace to a region scarred by war." The United States renewed its military commitment to protect the independence of Kosovo and pledged an additional $400 million in debt relief to the Kosovar government. In return, Bush was hailed as a national hero by the Kosovars and he even had a street named after him.

In this light, it is hard to imagine that the United States could refuse to respect the decision of Texas, or any State, that wished to leave the Union, so long as it reflected the popular will of the people and was done within the existing republican framework of governance.

In determining the process that Texas should use to facilitate an exit from the Union, it is common to look back to the Declaration of Independence in 1776 or the Texas Declaration of Independence in 1836 for guidance. While it is easy to draw inspiration from these documents, they offer no real, actionable assistance in this instance. As unilateral declarations of independence, they represent a process where every existing legal remedy had been exhausted and the only remedy remaining to preserve the right of self-government and fundamental liberties was revolution. That is not the situation for Texas. At least not yet.

In addition, a thorough examination of the process surrounding the creation of both declarations and the subsequent actions sparked by them finds that each was a product of the day and age in which it was written and was very specific to the circumstances under which it occurred. It is perfectly acceptable, however, to invoke the principles that inspired them.

Echoing the founders of the Republic of Texas in 1836, and Houston in 1861, nearly every instance of nations seeking self-determination in the latter half of the 20th century and the beginning of the 21st has hinged on a referendum. The reason is simple. If nations are comprised of people, fundamental changes in political relationships and the structure of governance should not be carried out by representatives. Rather, the people should individually represent themselves.

There is a certain reluctance to embrace the power of referendum on the part of those who fall on the conservative end of the spectrum. It is especially so here in Texas, where any attempt to implement a general framework for citizen-initiated referendum is immediately denounced and swiftly defeated. In its general form, the Republican Party of Texas has come out against granting the people direct access to the power of general referendum in its platform.

Texas does, however, conduct a state-sponsored referendum every two years. In November of odd-numbered years, constitutional amendments passed by the Texas Legislature are placed before the voters of Texas for their approval or rejection. This is a referendum. In fact, Texas voters have more experience with referenda than they might imagine. Over 320 Texas cities, classified as Home Rule Cities, have the power of referendum and exercise that power regularly. All local school districts hold referenda in the form of hotly debated school bond and tax elections.

The current Texas Constitution, while not explicitly establishing a framework for referenda, definitely reserves the right to make fundamental changes to how Texas is governed exclusively to the people. Article 1, Section 2 lays the right and responsibility squarely at the feet of the people of Texas to make fundamental changes in governance.

In every example cited in this work where a Western-style democratic society has achieved independence, the people, in their capacity as a body politic, have had the final say on their political destiny. In every instance, the very act of a referendum has clarified the political realities, pitting the people who want their voices heard against a political class who believe that they are, in fact, the ruling class in a de facto oligarchy. The very process of even attempting to obtain a referendum makes clear those battle lines and, more specifically, the people and institutions on each side. Those who oppose even having a referendum are, in reality, opposing the foundational principles of Texas and the United States, the people, and the democratic cornerstone of Western civilization. In short, anyone opposed to having a referendum on the issue of self-government is un-Texan and un-American.

LEGISLATIVE PATH

As previously stated, there is no existing statutory framework in Texas law specifically for conducting an independence referendum. There doesn't have to be. All the pieces are currently there. They just have to be assembled in the one place where it matters—the Texas Legislature.

This comes in the form of a standard bill. It's important to note that the Texas Legislature is a true part-time legislative body. They meet for exactly 140 days every other year unless called into a special session by the governor. In that 140-day period, they file and debate legislation over nearly every conceivable issue that impacts Texans. The Legislature files way more bills than ever get passed and it takes considerable work ahead of a legislative session to get enough momentum behind a bill to even give it a shot at passage.

The process begins by having the bill filed by a member of the House or Senate, plus a sponsor in the chamber opposite from the member who initially filed it. From there, it gets its first reading on the floor and is assigned to a committee. The committee chair schedules it for a hearing; sometimes they don't if they are opposed to the bill, and it dies when the session ends. But, if the committee hears the bill and it is voted out of committee, it gets scheduled to be heard on the floor, or it doesn't. The House and Senate each have their own rules for scheduling bills for the floor and, as has been the case in the Texas House, the chair of the Calendars Committee can use his or her power to kill a bill by refusing to move it along.

However, if it moves along, it gets debated on the floor and is then voted on. If it passes in one chamber, it moves to the other chamber and the process repeats until the bill is passed by both houses. At the end of the day, what any bill needs to pass is the support of 76 members of the

Texas House, 16 members of the Texas Senate, the lieutenant governor, and the governor. From there it moves to the governor's desk for his signature or a veto. While this may seem overly complicated, I assure you that it is actually more so. Yet every session the Texas Legislature manages to pass well over one thousand bills into law.

Snapper Carr, general counsel for Focused Advocacy LLC, described it this way:

> Despite the recent growth in the number of proposed pieces of legislation, the overall Texas legislative process is setup to produce "limited" government. The very fact that the Legislature is limited to meeting in Regular Session every other year is the first sign of the commitment that the framers of the Texas Constitution had to a narrow part-time citizen government. Every step of the legislative process is designed to weed out or consolidate various pieces of proposed legislation. Overall, the historical passage rate for filed legislation is approximately 20%, said another way 80% of all proposed bills fail.

Like it or not, this is the recognized constitutional process for the passage of legislation in Texas and, as such, it must be followed to the letter.

THE ELEMENTS OF AN INDEPENDENCE REFERENDUM

In a very basic sense, any independence referendum legislation must address four fundamental issues: the specific question and responses that will be posed to voters; who is eligible to vote in the referendum; when the vote will happen and where voting is conducted; and the percentage threshold of success for either side.

When it comes to the actual legislation for a Texit referendum, much of what is needed already exists in Texas law. There are plenty of laws already on the books that deal with the actual mechanics of voting. The Texas Election Code already specifies who is eligible to vote, how polling locations are chosen, the general conduct of state-wide elections and voting, and the currently accepted dates and times for statewide elections. In addition, Texas law is fairly clear that, when votes are placed to the people as a whole, the victory goes to the simple majority. All of these elements exist as part of our republican form of government with one major exception—the question.

The issue of how to pose the actual question to voters has caused quite a bit of hand wringing in other independence referenda around the world. In Scotland's lead-up to its independence referendum, the issue of how to word the question placed before voters was left up to the Scottish Parliament. They chose the yes or no question: "Do you agree that Scotland should be an independent country?" The U.K.'s Electoral Commission did some testing of the Scottish government's proposed wording. Citing concerns that the phrase "Do you agree" was not neutral enough and elicited a higher number of 'Yes' votes from those who were asked the question, the commission recommended altering the wording of the question to: "Should Scotland be an independent country?" This was the question that eventually appeared on the ballot.

This was again an issue in the lead-up to the Brexit vote. A June 2016 article on CNBC.com highlighted the importance behind the construction of the ballot language.

> *Subtle differences in the phrasing of a question or the response options can have a significant effect on polling results. Specific wording on a ballot has stirred debates on issues ranging from legalizing marijuana to same-sex marriage. One ballot question ended up in court in California following disagreements over the language used.*

> *"Frames have consequences," Gail Fairhurst, author of "The Power of Framing" told CNBC. "Mentioning only one side of the debate implicitly marginalizes the other side, treating it as a less than equal alternative."*

> *Social scientists often refer to it as framing theory and have researched how something is presented will influence the choices people make about how to process the information.*

While the Brexit question was changed from requiring a simple 'yes' or 'no' response to one that more accurately reflected how each side of the issue was perceived ('leave' and 'remain'), there was an enormous amount of thought and energy put into this seemingly simple aspect of the process.

It is important that the question placed before the voters of Texas accurately reflects the choice that people are being asked to make. In the case of Texas, the question must be asked in the context of its direct effect and framed as a choice between reasserting its previous status as an independent, self-governing nation-state or simply doing nothing.

SPECIAL CONSIDERATIONS

Outside of the basic requirements for an independence referendum, other issues should be considered. No two independence referenda are exactly alike. Most of the variation comes from significant differences in electoral systems and political culture. The rest is often a function of the political climate under which the vote is held.

A good example of this is how Catalonia had to improvise and move polling locations due to the threat by the Spanish central government to arrest anyone who helped carry out the referendum. Another was the push in Scotland to lower the voting age to 16 specifically for their independence referendum, their rationale being that the decision being made would significantly affect this age group and, therefore, they should have a say in making it.

In a Texit referendum, there are some additional considerations, unique to the circumstances of Texas, that warrant discussion and possible inclusion in any referendum legislation.

The first of these deals with campaign finance. As it stands, Texas has no limits on campaign contributions and campaign spending. Nor does it have any limitations on campaign contributions from outside of Texas other than a prohibition on "foreign" contributions. Given what is known about the role that money plays in traditional political campaigns, that role is likely to be exponentially magnified in a Texit campaign. In addition, it is reasonable to assume that a minimum of $1 billion dollars of outside money will pour into Texas from outside pro-federal interest groups opposed to Texit.

For a Texit referendum to accurately reflect the will of the people of Texas, there should be a strict prohibition of campaign funds originating from outside of Texas. In this case, spending from General Purpose Political Action Committees should be prohibited as well. Campaign spending should be restricted to Texas residents only or Political Action Committees established exclusively for this referendum. Texas may want to follow the example of the U.K. during the Brexit vote and set maximum spending caps on each campaign to ensure that each side of the debate gets heard equally by all Texans.

There is another major concern for Texas voters that should be taken into account. As of this writing, evidence is surfacing on an alarmingly regular basis that Texans have been the victims of serious voter fraud and have been so for years. As reported by Direct Action Texas, "data from the Texas Senate Research Center and Texas Legislative Council showed that 249 out of 254 counties had discrepancies between the number of votes and the number of voters in the 2016 primary."

In fact, a recent investigation by the Texas attorney general into 2016 election irregularities in Hill County stated these irregularities are likely to happen again. The attorney general's comment on the matter should be of particular concern in a Texit referendum. "This case highlights that inadequate safeguards exist to prevent such errors in future elections."

The widespread use of electronic voting machines in Texas may be convenient, but their mishandling has created an active breeding ground for election mismanagement and voter fraud. Therefore, Texans should strongly consider specifying that any Texit referendum be conducted exclusively by paper ballot. It might be slower to count, but it adds a degree of certainty to the results that simply cannot be produced by electronic voting.

Additionally, Texas should consider adopting a provision in any referendum legislation similar to one that became a major factor in the Brexit debate. A provision of the U.K. Referendum Act required the government to prepare official reports for the voters clarifying the relationship between the U.K. and the EU in key areas as well as identifying where the U.K. had attempted reforms in the EU and the result of each attempt.

Legislation similar to this regularly passes the Texas Legislature every session. Known as "study bills," they often direct state agencies to study the impacts and effects of various issues. Ahead of any debate on the issue, it is important that every Texan be given access to the data necessary to make an informed decision. Understanding the true relationship between Texas and the federal government with respect to the obligations of Texas under the current system, and seeing them compared with the obligations of other self-governing nation-states under agreements with the United States, can only serve to give voters a much clearer perspective on the issue.

It's not even necessary that these studies be part of referendum legislation. They could be passed as standalone items. However, integrating them into a referendum bill make them a part of the process, thereby giving their results an added degree of importance.

Texas should strongly consider what could and should happen in the event that individuals or institutions break the law regarding the referendum. The punishment for those who break campaign finance laws currently amounts to a slap on the wrist. The penalties for voter fraud are a bit stiffer. However, in the context of a Texit referendum, offenses such as these can have an outsized impact, transforming them from misdemeanors to major crimes against the people of Texas.

Given the passion that currently exists on both sides of the Texit issue, which will no doubt continue to grow in the lead-up to a referendum, the potential is high that some of those who support the status quo may resort to breaking the law in order to scuttle the vote. This is especially true if they sense ahead of the vote that they are going to be on the losing side. In the absence of stronger safeguards and harsh penalties, it wouldn't be unexpected to see ballot stuffing, voter suppression, voter fraud, and a whole host of other dirty tricks.

Therefore, a deterrent to these types of illegal behavior should be included in referendum legislation. Enhancing criminal penalties already in place and enacting criminal penalties for blatant campaign finance violations relating to the referendum would be a start. However, some may see criminal penalties as their personal sacrifice to prevent Texit. In this case, it would be prudent to stipulate that, if there is any evidence of a significant amount of voter fraud or campaign finance irregularities, an automatic re-vote will be triggered within 180 days and anyone convicted of voter fraud or campaign finance irregularities should jointly bear the cost of the re-vote.

Finally, any referendum legislation should include a deadline for negotiations and transition to be completed on key issues subsequent to an affirmative vote for Texit. At a minimum, it must include timetables for concrete action from Texas officials. Few things motivate better than a deadline.

When Britain triggered Article 50 of the Lisbon Treaty, the treaty that governs the European Union, it initiated a two-year period for negotiation and transition. Regardless of the outcome of any formal negotiations, at the end of the two-year period, the U.K. would no longer be a member of the European Union. This deadline looms large over both the Eurocrats and the elected leaders in the U.K. It is a prime motivator, on both sides, to get any outstanding issues in relation to their new status as peers worked out in a timely manner, because "no deal" is still a deal.

A Texit referendum should be no different. However, there is an important caveat. Unlike the U.K.'s vote to leave the EU, a vote for independence in a Texit referendum is a mandate for Texas to begin the process of asserting independence. Although desirable, it does not require the participation or cooperation of any entity outside of Texas.

Regardless of the response from the federal government, in the absence of negotiated agreements with the United States, the Texas government should be on a timetable to move forward.

THE BILL

Ahead of the 2013 legislative session, members of the TNM aggressively lobbied to get a non-binding independence referendum bill filed. The proposed legislation was extremely basic, containing a slew of "whereas" statements explaining the grievances against the federal government and explaining the constitutional rationale for a vote. But it ended with the words every Texit advocate wants to see.

Therefore, be it Resolved by the Senate and House of Representatives of the State of Texas assembled, that a plebiscite be conducted at the next regularly scheduled Constitutional amendment election to determine the will of the citizens of the State of Texas regarding the independence of Texas.

Be it further Resolved that:

The vote of the citizens on the issue of independence be non-binding and advisory only.

That the results of the voting of the citizens of Texas be reported to the Governor and the sitting members of the Legislature of the State of Texas for further consideration in accordance with the wishes of the citizens of the State of Texas.

That the results of the voting also be reported to both houses of the United States Congress and the President of the United States.

That the wording of the issue to be placed on the ballot shall be as follows: 'The State of Texas should reassert its status as an independent nation.'

Notwithstanding the fact that very few people, including elected representatives, are familiar with the term plebiscite, the effect of this legislation, if passed, seemed obvious to Texit advocates. The problem was that the proposed bill wasn't really a bill at all, a fact that was used to great effect by the Texas Legislative Council.

Unknown to most Texans, virtually every piece of legislation proposed by legislators first goes to the Texas Legislative Council. According to its website, officially it is "a nonpartisan legislative agency that provides bill drafting, computing, research, publishing, and document distribution services to the Texas Legislature and the other legislative agencies." Unofficially, it serves as legislative gatekeeper, formatting and reworking submitted legislation to standardize format and avoid inconsistencies within existing law. In this instance, they assumed the role of the Texas Supreme Court.

State Representative James White courageously agreed to file the proposal, and it became House Concurrent Resolution 77. On its face, it was exactly what Texit advocates wanted. HCR 77 spelled out a defense of state sovereignty under both the U.S. and Texas Constitutions and highlighted key grievances with the federal government. However, there was one notable exception. The referendum language had been completely stripped out.

When challenged with the fact that it now amounted to nothing more than a list of complaints with no substance, White explained that the Texas Legislative Council was concerned that the referendum language would have been illegal and removed it. In retrospect, they were right, but for the wrong reasons. The proposed legislation, specifically the language about the referendum, was too generic and lacked any references to existing statute.

However, with a much clearer understanding of the process, as well as the current statutory framework, it becomes a simple matter to combine all of these elements to see what an actual Texas Independence Referendum Act would look like. Amazingly, the legislation required to initiate a Texit referendum is incredibly simple when contemplating the large impact it will have.

The Texas Independence Referendum Act
A BILL TO BE ENTITLED
AN ACT
to make provision for the holding of a referendum on whether Texas should reassert its status as an independent nation.
BE IT ENACTED BY THE LEGISLATURE OF THE STATE OF TEXAS:

SECTION 1. Title 16 of the Election Code is amended by adding Chapter 279 to read as follows:

CHAPTER 279. TEXAS INDEPENDENCE REFERENDUM

SUBCHAPTER A. REFERENDUM

Sec. 279.001 THE REFERENDUM

(1) A referendum is to be held on whether Texas should reassert its status as an independent nation or remain a member of the United States.

(2) The referendum shall be held on the next regularly scheduled general election date after the passage of this act and any subsequent general elections dates as called by the Governor, a 2/3rds vote of the Texas Legislature or upon the submission of a petition of Texas voters in accordance with chapter 172 of the Texas Election Code.

(3) The day appointed under subsection (2) must be no later than 31 December 2018.

(4) The question that is to appear on the ballot is—

"Should the State of Texas reassert its status as an independent nation?"

(5) The alternative answers to that question that are to appear on the ballot are—

"Yes" and "No".

Sec. 279.002 DUTY TO PUBLISH INFORMATION ON OUTCOME OF PREVIOUS EFFORTS TO REFORM THE FEDERAL UNION AND ASSERT TEXAS SOVEREIGNTY

(1) The Secretary of State must publish a report which contains (alone or with other material)—

(a) a statement which details previous efforts by the State of Texas to initiate reform in the relationship between the State of Texas and the Federal union as well as efforts to retain or reassert the sovereignty of the State of Texas, and

(b) the opinion of the Secretary of State on the success of those efforts.

(2) The report must be published no later than 10 weeks before the scheduled referendum date.

(3) A copy of the report published under this section must be submitted to the Legislature of the State of Texas, the Governor, the Lieutenant Governor, the Texas Congressional delegation, and the President of the United States.

Sec. 279.003 DUTY TO PUBLISH INFORMATION ABOUT TEXAS MEMBERSHIP IN THE UNITED STATES

(1)The Secretary of State must publish a report which contains (alone or with other material)—

(a) information about rights and obligations of the State of Texas and its citizens that arise under Federal law as a result of Texas membership in the United States, and

(b) examples of countries that are not part of the United States but do have other arrangements and agreements with the United States (describing, in the case of each country given as an example, those arrangements).

(2) The report must be published no later than 10 weeks before the scheduled referendum date.

(3) A copy of the report published under this section must be submitted to the Legislature of the State of Texas, the Governor, the Lieutenant Governor, the Texas Congressional delegation, and the President of the United States.

Sec. 279.004 CAMPAIGN CONTRIBUTIONS AND EXPENDITURES FOR THIS REFERENDUM

(1) For the purposes of this referendum,

Campaign expenditures shall only be made from funds contributed by eligible Texas voters.

Only political action committees registered in Texas no later than 6 months after this legislation takes effect shall be allowed to make campaign expenditures.

No campaign expenditure can be made from the campaign

account of any current or former elected official or from any specific purpose political action committee unrelated to this referendum.

All offenses committed under this section and Chapter 253 are enhanced to State Jail Felonies.

Other than these specific provisions, all sections of Chapter 253 apply to campaign contributions and expenditures for this referendum.

Sec. 279.005 RESULTS OF THE REFERENDUM

(1) The results of the referendum shall be reported first and foremost to the citizens of Texas, to both houses of the United States Congress and to the President of the United States by the Governor of the State of Texas.

(2) Should the vote of the citizens result in a YES decision for Texas independence, the Texas Legislature shall, within twelve calendar months following the referendum, craft an Ordinance for Texas Independence defining and outlining a plan to implement the decision of the referendum, to include an operational plan, to establish Texas as an independent republic.

While this language is, in and of itself, a complete bill that could be filed in the next session of the Texas Legislature, it should only be treated as a starting point and not a finished product. There should be plenty of deliberation on the framework for the referendum, but it should not be victim of "paralysis by analysis."

THE DEBATE

Leading up to the passage of the referendum bill and through to the actual vote, the debate will be vigorous. However, until there is a vote, there will be no honest debate on the issue of Texas. To quote Weston Martinez, "You have to have the vote to have the conversation."

Ultimately, the success or failure of Texit at the polls will be determined by the scope of the debate and the strategy used by each side to convince Texans to choose to leave or remain. In any debate on Texit, the side advocating for maintaining the status quo has a near insurmountable task. They essentially have to argue that all of the reasons that created enough political momentum to actually have a vote to leave still aren't bad enough to leave. This puts them in the unenviable position of having to dismiss the legitimate concerns of virtually every Texan. At a minimum, if they acknowledge that legitimate concerns exist, they have to show that there is a reasonable and viable path to addressing these concerns within the federal system. Again, given the attitude that Texas voters have about the feasibility of reforming the federal system, this puts them at a severe disadvantage.

This is why, so often, you see the advocates of the status quo attempting to redirect the debate to focus voters on the uncertainty posed by abandoning the status quo. By shifting the debate in this way, it baits those who are seeking self-determination into explicitly declaring post-independence policies that are then tied to the referendum. For those advocating for Texit, it is important to avoid this pitfall that became a major factor in the rejection of independence by Scottish voters.

One of the biggest mistakes made by the Scottish National Party in the 2014 Scottish independence referendum came in the form of a white paper produced by the SNP-dominated government, called

Scotland's Future. The purpose of the 670-page tome was to create, in the words of First Minister Alex Salmond, the "most comprehensive blueprint for an independent country ever published."

Within its pages, it attempted to do that very thing. It contained 200 pages of answers to the most commonly asked questions about Scottish independence, and specifically addressed some of the more complex issues related to citizenship, travel, currency, and debt. However, it went further by advocating for post-independence policies that were staples of SNP campaigns in Scotland for years. This is where it went off the rails. While many hailed the ambition of the document and lauded the effort for moving the independence conversation forward, others, particularly voters, saw it more as a post-independence SNP election manifesto.

With the publication of the white paper, the debate over Scotland's independence shifted. The points of contention no longer centered on the viability and practicality of an independent Scotland. Rather, the conversation became infinitely more complicated as the focus of contention became about the post-independence policies of the SNP.

Sensing an opening, the Better Together campaign pounced on an opportunity to tie the entire issue of Scotland's independence on the governance of the SNP and the popularity of its specific policy positions. Suddenly their messaging shifted from "independence is a bad idea" to "a vote for independence is a vote for the SNP."

The SNP was then forced into a two-front war, having to defend its policies while simultaneously trying to advocate for independence. After all, that's what political parties do. They advance policy proposals based on the principles of their party. In doing so, the SNP fell into a trap of its own making and subverted the most attractive benefit of independence —the opportunity to create something new.

They promised a concrete, fixed future that didn't yet exist and created in the minds of the voters the notion that Scottish independence was merely an extension of current SNP governance. The voters were aware of what the future looked like if they stayed in the United Kingdom. The boundless and unlimited opportunity presented by the right of self-government, to remake the future in their image, was stolen from Scottish voters by the introduction of the white paper.

I firmly believe that, while not the primary cause of the defeat of the Scottish referendum, this played a major role in the final result. The clue is in the numbers. The SNP received 44.04 percent of the votes in the 2011 Scottish Parliament elections. The 'Yes' vote in the 2014 independence referendum received 44.7 percent.

If the majority of Texit advocates can avoid this trap, they are in the proverbial "cat bird seat." However, this debate will not be the normal partisan bickering we are all used to. It will create very strange bedfellows as the battle lines become clearly drawn. For Texit to win the debate, it will have to be able to clearly articulate why staying in the Union is no longer an option and, with exceptional discipline, key in on the opportunity that can exist in an independent Texas, promising nothing other than giving Texans their first chance at self-government in their entire lives. Given the broad patchwork of people and interests that will be working for Texit, all would do well to remember the saying, "Only a fool fights in a burning house."

THE WIN

The current threshold to win any vote in Texas is a simple majority of those who vote. While there are examples of greater thresholds around the world related to political separation, such as the imposition by the Canadian Supreme Court of an arbitrary 55 percent threshold for Quebec to exit, there is no similar precedent in Texas for popular votes. There is no question or debate about that aspect of the referendum. Rather, what's more interesting is predicting the number of votes that will be required to win.

Since the threshold to win a Texit vote is a simple majority, it will take 50 percent plus 1 of those who cast a vote in the referendum. In the modern-day independence referenda, voter turnout is exceptional. In some instances, over 90 percent of those who are eligible to vote do so. The Scottish referendum turnout of 84.6 percent was the highest recorded for an election or referendum in the United Kingdom since the introduction of universal suffrage. The voter turnout for the Brexit referendum was 72.2 percent. The message is clear: when people finally get a real choice on the ballot, they show up.

By estimating a high-average 85 percent or higher voter turnout, we can calculate the number of votes it will take for Texit to carry the day. With 15,101,087 currently registered voters in Texas, the number of votes required to win is likely to be between 6,417,963 and 7,550,544. To put that figure in perspective, that is slightly less than all votes cast for all presidential candidates in the 2016 general election.

Like all elections, it will all come down to retail politics, excelling in the fundamentals of getting the message out and getting voters to the polls. Whichever side does it most effectively will win the day. Nigel Farage, former leader of the U.K. Independence Party, on the eve of the Brexit referendum, summarized what it would take to win.

"The Leave side can only win if we have an effective ground campaign comprising of activists from across the political spectrum working together."

The Texit campaign will be no different. While the Texit referendum will be hard fought, the numbers, the momentum, and the strength of the Texit argument point to a win. When Texans wake up on the morning following the vote, they will face a new world in which the reality of self-government is in their hands. There will be celebrations and excitement and then Texans will get to work creating their future.

7 | BECOMING INDEPENDENT

66 The future is all around us, waiting in moments of transition, to be born in moments of revelation. No one knows the shape of that future, or where it will take us. 99

J. Michael Straczynski

On June 24, 2016, the people of Britain awoke to a nightmare. Following the official announcement that the people had voted to leave the European Union, chaos reigned. BBC viewers turned on their televisions to witness a death match between Nigel Farage, clad only in a studded leather thong, and a mohawked Prime Minister David Cameron in the hastily constructed Brexitdome. Everywhere, Britons were hustling to earn the new currency of a post-Brexit United Kingdom—jars of Marmite. Violent protesters stormed Buckingham Palace, demanding that the image of the queen on the British pound be replaced by the moon-faced visage of Benny Hill, the poster child for post-Brexit anarchy.

It would have been a dramatic spectacle had it actually happened. To listen to the pundits and the naysayers, this was the best-case scenario. What actually happened was far less dramatic. The most dramatic after effects came in the economic sector. The British pound initially slipped in value against the euro and the dollar, which prompted more foreign spending in the U.K., leading to a record rise in retail sales. The FTSE 250, the stock exchange of the 250 biggest companies in the U.K., fell 13 percent in the two days after the vote came in, only to close up 3.7 percent for the entire year. The FTSE closed 2016 in record territory, making it Europe's best-performing major stock market for the year.

Much has been made of the difficulties that would be faced by the people of Texas in the event of a successful independence referendum. Rather than being grounded in the reality of what actually happened in similar circumstances, the crumbling hellscape is the picture the pundits want to paint for a post-referendum Texas. The prognosticators paint a picture of a world that resembles a cross between the Australian wastelands of a Mad Max movie and the apocalyptic visions of John the Revelator.

Behind the dystopian post-referendum nightmares of political pundits lies the reality. In the immediate aftermath of an affirmative Texas independence vote, things continue as they have until they don't. The mail gets delivered. The trash gets picked up. Goods flow. Money is earned and spent. Literally, nothing changes until it does.

While this may be a surprise to some, their surprise stems from a fundamental misunderstanding of the independence process. Independence is not a single act embodied in a referendum. Independence is a state of being. The referendum is the first step in the process, an expression of political will that kicks off the process of becoming independent. It is, however, an important step. Such an expression of political will must be respected. It demands action. However, that action must be balanced with care and caution as Texas enters the next phase—negotiation and transition.

There should be one single aim for relations with the United States in the immediate aftermath of Texit—minimizing disruption. While those opposed to Texit would love to think that disruption cannot be avoided or even mitigated as Texas leaves the Union, they are dead wrong. In fact, the tools necessary to effect a speedy, efficient, and minimally disruptive Texit are already at our disposal. Before discussing what specific measures could or should be taken after a referendum, it's important to take stock of these tools and examine how 195 independent, self-governing nation-states already operate, especially regarding one another.

Modern, self-governing, Western-style nation-states typically use four mechanisms to conduct the business of state. Fundamental issues of governance are addressed in a constitution that, if it's already in existence and contains a method to do so, can be changed through amendments. In the case of Texas, the existing State constitution is already in the form of a republic with a form that is virtually identical to that of an independent nation-state.

Nations, at least those that are republics, have legislative bodies that makes laws under the authorization of the aforementioned constitution. The executive branch of the government can execute administrative actions that affect the operations of its various departments and agencies and set the rules for how the laws are executed. The final set of tools in the arsenal are international agreements that come in either the form of bilateral agreements between two countries or standing multilateral agreements to which more than two countries have signed on.

These tools of statecraft are important to understanding the mechanisms that can be used to transition from being a member State of the United States to an independent nation-state. However, one other component is helpful in understanding how a transition will play out. There is a major shift in the mindset that follows a referendum outcome in favor of Texit. From the moment the vote is certified, Texas and the United States become, for all intents and purposes, foreign to one another. Texans must begin to view the United States and its government no differently than any other foreign government or supranational entity. Negotiating with the federal government becomes like negotiating with Mexico or the United Nations.

There are highly probable scenarios where the outcome of Texas leaving the Union is smooth with virtually no disruption. After all, it is in the best interests of both Texas and the United States to ensure that disruption be kept to a minimum while respecting the decision of Texans to govern themselves. The scenarios I present here are the ones that are the most fair to both parties and the easiest to implement. They use existing legal mechanisms, federal policies, and international norms and institutions that currently govern the relationship between the United States and other countries. Most importantly, they acknowledge the fact that, just because Texans now keep their government closer to home, doesn't mean Texas and the United States have to be adversaries. The point, however, is not to say with absolute certainty what will happen. Instead, it's to show what can and should happen in light of what already exists and what is already happening.

FIRST THINGS FIRST

Before Texit negotiations with the federal government can begin in earnest, there is one important step Texas needs to take at home. In fact, without it, negotiation and transition are impossible. That step is a constitutional makeover.

There have been some voices in the Texit debate that insist there can be no Texit without first having drafted and ratified a new constitution for an independent Republic of Texas. Given the unwieldy size of the current Texas Constitution, there might be some merit to revisiting it. However, the assertion that no Texit can take place without it is completely wrong. In fact, without some changes to the existing constitution, post-referendum, the Texas government doesn't possess the legal authority or the statutory framework to move to the next step.

The problem is basic. There is no legal framework for Texas to engage the United States on equal footing. The legal framework that currently exists allows Texas to engage the other States within the Union, but nothing that allows Texas to engage them all as a collective entity. As a State of the Union, we are prohibited from entering into treaties under Article 1, Section 10 of the United States Constitution. This is problematic, as a significant portion of the negotiation and transition will require Texas to sit across the negotiating table with representatives of the United States, as well as other countries, as equals to execute international agreements on a variety of issues.

Luckily, in the wake of an affirmative vote for Texit, Texas has the power to make the needed changes to the Texas Constitution required to start the process without rewriting the entire document. In the 1960s, a complete overhaul of the Texas Constitution was completed through what became known as the Deadwood Amendment. It was a single constitutional amendment that removed redundant or obsolete language from the Texas Constitution. Some of these provisions dealt with land issues related to Spanish land grants. Some dealt with cleaning up language that existed elsewhere in the Constitution or had been overturned by the courts. All these edits and changes were rolled into a single constitutional amendment and placed before the voters of Texas.

In a similar fashion, any substantial constitutional changes required because of the independent status of Texas can be accomplished in this way without requiring a constitutional convention. This would include changing the official name of Texas from the "State of Texas" to the "Republic of Texas," as well as removing references to the United States, the federal government, and the federal Constitution. It should also include changing the names of elected positions in Texas government to reflect its new national character. For example, it could rename the office of governor to president and the legislature to congress. While these are somewhat cosmetic changes, the most significant change will include redefining the role of the Texas secretary of state and expanding the duties of the office to include international relations.

The most important addition, however, will be the addition of a constitutional provision granting treaty-making authority to the Texas government and defining the process under which treaties are proposed and ratified.

At some point early in this phase of the process, Texas will also have to deal with some gaps in current State statutes. While there is an equivalent State-level agency to nearly every federal-level agency, making the transition of executive and administrative functions much easier, there are likely some holes in the legal framework. We see an example of this right now as the U.K. vigorously debates legislation in this regard because of its exit from the European Union. A by-product of being in a political and economic union for an extended period is that, in many instances, the member states of a political union defer to the laws and regulations of that union in certain areas. Therefore, laws at the state level that are equivalent to those at the federal level simply have never been written and do not exist in the newly independent nation-state.

The U.K. has chosen to address these gaps through a single, comprehensive piece of legislation that will enact many of these laws and regulations. However, while Texas may wish to follow suit, there is an equally good chance that the low-regulation, small-government attitude of Texas will look at this as an opportunity to simply end many of the regulations, laws, and programs that only exist in Texas due to the imposition of the federal superstate.

However Texas chooses to address it, underlying it all is a clean slate. It is an opportunity for Texas to begin to shape its government and policy to address the fundamental challenges that Texans will face in the very early stages of Texit.

Once this is accomplished, negotiation and transition can begin in earnest. It is important to point out that negotiation and transition aren't actually separate processes. They work in concert. As each issue is negotiated and an agreement is reached, that agreement moves the transition process forward until there are no issues left to resolve and Texas is as independent as it wants to be.

If the groundwork was properly laid in the referendum, then there should be a firm deadline on the resolution of all these transitional issues. There has to be a fixed point where both parties either agree on the key issues or agree to disagree and move on without agreement, each operating in their own interests, just not at that time and not necessarily with one another. Nothing does that better than a fixed date for exit.

In this negotiation with the United States, there are a handful of major areas that will have to be addressed. These are trade, travel, banking and currency, Social Security, defense, and Texas' portion of the national debt. Of these, only Social Security, defense, and national debt require exclusive and unique agreements with the United States, and defense only on a very limited subset of issues. The others are all areas where agreements will also have to be forged with other countries anyway as a natural byproduct of being an independent nation.

TRADE

Trade is the major issue that has the clearest path to resolution with the United States and it is one of the most important. International trade is a major driver of the Texas economy. In fact, Texas exports products to virtually every country in the world with the total value of exports to just the top 25 totaling between $225 and $285 billion every single year. These are just the figures for products that originate in Texas and doesn't include imports that flow through our ports and travel across our roads every day. Trade is major.

It is important to examine how trade works between Texas and the rest of the States and then see if there is a fair path to approximate that relationship now that gives Texas some control over the situation.

Currently, Texas is restricted in external trade by the prohibitions on States in Article 1, Section 10 of the U.S. Constitution, fully vesting that authority in the U.S. Congress. Consequently, States have little to no control over the flow of goods and services across their borders and there are certainly no trade tariffs between the States. Within the United States, member States have tariff-free trade and a singular external trade policy. Not accounting for the common currency, this economic relationship between the States is the textbook definition of a customs union. Some would argue that the United States is a fully integrated economic union, but the States retain a large degree of control over their individual fiscal policies, meaning that the United States is not a true economic union.

It is important to note that, other than the United States, there are 13 other customs unions around the world comprising virtually all of Central America, South America, nearly all of Europe and portions of the old Soviet Union, and major blocs of countries in Africa and the Arabian Peninsula. In these customs unions, independent self-governing countries conduct trade in the same way as the States of the United States without being in a political union.

The clearest and easiest way to ensure that there is absolutely no disruption of trade between the U.S. and an independent Texas is for the two to enter into a customs union, but as equals. Anyone who thinks this would be unusual or far-fetched simply doesn't understand the way trade works. Most people believe that the only free trade agreement the U.S. is a part of is the multilateral North American Free Trade Agreement (NAFTA) between the U.S., Canada, and Mexico. It's not. The U.S. also has free trade agreements with Australia, Bahrain, Chile, Colombia, Costa Rica, Dominican Republic, El Salvador, Guatemala, Honduras, Israel, Jordan, Korea, Morocco, Nicaragua, Oman, Panama, Peru, and Singapore, all of which have a smaller GDP than Texas.

A negotiated trade agreement between Texas and the U.S., either through a customs union or a free trade agreement, would ensure continued tariff-free trade between the two. Any agreement should ensure continued access to rail lines, airports, seaports, and highways for the transportation of goods.

If the negotiated agreement is a customs union, the work is done. If, however, the U.S. or Texas opts for a free trade agreement instead, Texas would retain the freedom to pursue bilateral or multilateral trade agreements with any other nations without restriction. That includes negotiating trade agreements with countries that already have free trade agreements with the U.S., ensuring a continuity of trade policy.

In the event that Texas and the U.S. fail to come to terms, Texas could still trade with the U.S. using standard World Trade Organization tariff schedules and trade rules that have already been agreed to by the U.S. In short, Texas could take the tariff tables submitted to the WTO by the U.S., scratch out its name, write in ours, and submit it. This again leaves Texas the freedom to hammer out its own trade policies and trade with every country in the world, much like we are already doing, with one exception—it will be on our terms. In short, no matter how trade negotiations go with the U.S., Texas will be just fine.

TRAVEL

Invariably, when the debate about Texit comes up, someone offers what they believe is the question that should put the nail in the Texit coffin. "Will we need a passport to visit our family in Oklahoma?" The response should be that, if they still have family living in Oklahoma, they must not be setting a good enough example to entice their family to move to Texas. Although flippant answers would be much more enjoyable, the reality of how travel could work in a post-Texit world is so simple it's just quicker to give the real answer.

Negotiating travel between the United States and an independent Texas should be relatively easy since there is already an example of how the United States handles regular travel between itself and a contiguous foreign country. All we have to do is look south toward Mexico.

Starting in 2014, the number of people legally crossing the U.S.-Mexico border topped one million daily. Passports aren't even required, as the U.S. government allows Mexican citizens to use "Border Crossing Cards" to enter the United States from Mexico "by land, or by pleasure vessel or ferry."

There is a very good reason that motivates the federal government to lower the barriers to travel between contiguous countries and itself. It's good for the economy.

Noe Garcia, president of the Border Trade Alliance, singled out the economic motivator. "Legal border crossings at the dozens of ports of entries located along the U.S.-Mexican border significantly benefit both the U.S. and Mexican economies, which is why the numbers continue to rise."

However, anyone concerned about the use of passports to travel from State to State within the United States should hope they don't live in one of handful of States that haven't implemented the federal guidelines in 2005's REAL ID Act. Starting in January of 2018, residents of Kentucky, Maine, Minnesota, Missouri, Montana, Oklahoma, Pennsylvania, South Carolina, and Washington will need a passport to board any flight, domestic or international, according to new TSA guidelines. However, the States not listed have state-issued IDs that are compliant with the TSA guidelines. In addition, government-issued Border Crossing Cards and Global Entry Cards can be used.

This is all to point out that travel agreements between self-governing independent nations are common, as is the desire of nations to ease travel restrictions between those countries while maintaining high standards for security.

A great example of this is the federal Visa Waiver program that allows the citizens of certain countries to travel to and through the United States for up to 90 days for tourism or business without having to obtain a visa. That program includes Andorra, Australia, Austria, Belgium, Brunei, Chile, the Czech Republic, Denmark, Estonia, Finland, France, Germany, Greece, Hungary, Iceland, Ireland, Italy, Japan, Latvia, Liechtenstein, Lithuania, Luxembourg, Malta, Monaco, Netherlands, New Zealand, Norway, Portugal, San Marino, Singapore, Slovakia, Slovenia, South Korea, Spain, Sweden, Switzerland, Taiwan and the United Kingdom, with nine other countries in the process of being certified.

It is reasonable to assume that Texas would readily qualify for all existing programs instituted by the federal government that lower the barriers to travel and speed the process for those who travel. This would have to be discussed, and final agreements would be part of the negotiations.

In addition, during the transition, Texas would have to implement a system to fully manage the existing international border crossings or operate them jointly under an agreement with the federal government.

There is a precedent for a multilateral international agreement on common external border policy in the European Union, where there is free travel between member States because they share a common process for management of borders with non-EU members.

However, given the importance that Texans place on strengthening the border and creating a sensible border policy, it is likely that, beyond reducing travel barriers between Texas and the rest of the States, Texas will want as much control over the maintenance and security of its borders and points of entry as practically possible.

CURRENCY AND BANKING

One major benefit of Texit is, for the first time, Texas will have the opportunity for full control over our currency and monetary policy. The best part is that we can regain as much control over it as we want at a pace that makes sense for us. There is, however, one important consideration. Minimizing disruption during the transition out of the Union may initially dictate one course of action, while long-term financial stability for the new nation-state will likely require something different.

As a State, Texas has absolutely no control over monetary policy. While the United States Congress ostensibly has control over fiscal policy, monetary policy is solely determined by the pseudo-governmental Federal Reserve. Without consent or true oversight by elected representatives, they control the supply of currency, the flow of capital, and set the interest rates. In short, even through our participation in the governmental processes of the Union, we have virtually no say in monetary policy. Texit changes all of that.

Where Texas decides to go depends upon the degree of control we want over monetary policy. For this, we need to look at how other self-governing nations deal with the issue of currency.

When a nation-state first gains independence, in the absence of its own currency, it usually declares, unilaterally, the currency that is common to the region as its official currency. This is called an informal currency union. In the early days of independence, doing so provides for economic stability as consumers and businesses can continue to transact business in exactly the same way as they always have.

Where the U.S. dollar is concerned, its status as an international reserve currency has made it attractive to countries that have no desire to adopt their own currency. Many self-governing countries even allow the U.S. dollar to circulate freely in addition to their own currency.

According to a 2014 article on the website *Quartz*:

"The US dollar is the most widely used currency in the world, with many countries employing it as an accepted alternative to their own currency. But some have simply adopted the currency as their own, notes and all, in what is known as "dollarization." They don't have control over the currency—only the Federal Reserve in Washington sets monetary policy."

To be clear, this can be done without the blessing of the United States, as it has been in Ecuador, East Timor, El Salvador, Marshall Islands, Micronesia, Palau, Turks and Caicos, British Virgin Islands, and Zimbabwe.

If Texas wanted to have a say in monetary policy and still use the U.S. dollar, it would have to negotiate a formal currency union with the United States. Formal currency unions are common in the world; in fact, there are more than 20 official currency unions throughout the world. While a negotiated currency union with the United States would be desirable, the terms under which such an agreement could be executed likely would not give Texans any more control over monetary policy than we have now.

The most likely scenario is that Texas will adopt the U.S. dollar as its official currency in the immediate aftermath of a Texit vote to encourage stability while seeking a negotiated currency union with the United States. Depending on the terms of any negotiated agreement or in the absence of one, Texas will want to explore moving toward a currency of its own as soon as possible. Given the lack of long-term financial stability in the United States due to the exploding national debt, a Texas currency should come sooner rather than later.

Closely attached to the issue of currency is that of banking. Banking institutions are already covered by a regulatory regime that makes for a smooth transition during Texit. Existing federal law already allows foreign banks to operate in the United States through a direct banking office or a nonbanking representative office. Foreign banks also run standard consumer retail banks with their deposits insured by the Federal Deposit Insurance Corporation (FDIC), just like domestic banks. In fact, many large U.S. banks are owned by foreign banks.

In 2015, Bauer Financial, a Florida-based research firm, compiled a list of banks in the United States that are at least 25 percent foreign-owned, and identified 44 different banks operating in the United States. This list included the familiar full-service retail banks Compass and HSBC with 688 and 246 branches respectively.

Conversely, the State of Texas currently allows non-Texas banks to operate in Texas. In fact, Texas goes out of its way to ensure that operating a bank in Texas is as attractive as possible. Article XVI, Section 16(c) of the Texas Constitution provides that Texas-chartered state banks have the same rights and privileges that are or may be granted to national banks of the United States domiciled in Texas. This clause essentially gives banks an option to operate under a charter from the United States or from the State of Texas operating under the oversight of the Texas Department of Banking.

In July 1999, then Governor George W. Bush signed a bill into law that formally opened Texas to interstate bank branching. The bill made Texas bank charters one of the most attractive in the United States to conduct banking business. The bill included what was called the "super parity" provision, which provides a framework for a state bank chartered in Texas to conduct any of the activities allowed by any other insured state or federal financial institution anywhere else in the United States. This provision increases the value of existing state charters and increases Texas' appeal as a central location from which to conduct nationwide banking activities. In contrast, there is no "super parity" provision available to so-called national banks.

With the existing laws and regulations already in place, both in Texas and in the United States, banking is likely one of the areas that will be least affected by a Texit.

SOCIAL SECURITY

The Social Security issue is perhaps the thorniest and the most complex. If most Texans understood how the system currently worked, they would likely opt for open rebellion rather than an orderly Texit. Before looking at how Texas should handle this issue in the negotiation and transition phase, it is important to make an honest assessment of the Social Security system as it is now in the United States.

While Social Security retirement benefits are perceived as an earned benefit, in actuality the benefits paid are at the discretion of the federal government. It amounts to a government-sponsored, government-mandated Ponzi scheme that relies on an increasing number of workers who pay into the system in order to pay out the benefits promised by the self-serving political class.

The faith in the government's ability to meet its promises is eroding daily. A 2015 survey by Pew Research Center found that 41 percent of Americans think there will be no Social Security benefits for them when they retire. Another third believe they will receive significantly reduced levels of benefits.

In CNBC's article about the PRC report, they painted an even direr scenario.

"The Social Security and Medicare Trustees' 2014 report projects that all the Social Security trust funds will be depleted by 2033. At that point, the agency will be able to pay out about 77 percent of retirement benefits from payroll taxes collected. By 2088, the trustees forecast the agency will be able to pay out 72 percent of benefits. (Studies from Harvard and Dartmouth project the trust funds could be depleted sooner than that and claim the Social Security Administration's actuarial forecasts have been consistently overstating the financial health of the program's trust funds since 2000.)"

When contemplating the path forward in negotiating this aspect of Texit, it is important to keep in mind that the real possibility exists that Social Security retirement will disappear sooner rather than later. It is also important to think about current and future Texans who are forced to pay into a retirement system that could leave them destitute in their old age.

In a post-referendum Texit, Texas will need to think about Texans first and will have to advocate for them. While we can look for common ground in other areas of negotiation and seek opportunities for a win-win solution, when it comes to Social Security, Texas must take a "no surrender" approach.

Any Texan who has paid into the Social Security system and is currently receiving benefits should continue to receive them. This is non-negotiable. This was an obligation of the federal government to those who paid into the system and should, therefore, be met without question, hesitation, or reservation. This should be no problem for the federal government since it is possible for Social Security recipients to move to a foreign country and still collect their benefits. Additionally, those who have paid in should be able to preserve their accrued benefits for exactly the same reason.

To lessen the impact of a sudden change in the system, workers who are currently paying into that system should be given an option to continue paying into the United States Social Security system or opting out completely. It's safe to assume that many Texans will opt out and invest in private retirement accounts, but some will want to continue paying into the federal system, especially those close to retirement age. Given the reports of how dire the situation is for the Social Security Trust Fund, the federal government will likely find it appealing to have some Texans still paying into the system.

Moving forward, Texans may find it beneficial to establish a voluntary retirement and pension system similar to the one that already exists for state employees and educators. An easier step would be to open enrollment for either or both of those systems to any citizen in Texas.

Where the future relationship between Texas and the United States is concerned, this is more important than it might seem on its face. Post-Texit, there will be businesses that have feet in both Texas and the United States. Those businesses will want to seamlessly transfer workers from one place to the other without potentially subjecting them to dual Social Security taxation, the situation that occurs when a worker from one country works in another country and is required to pay Social Security taxes to both countries on the same earnings.

This is accomplished by the execution of what are known as international totalization agreements. Totalization agreements allow workers to combine the years they have worked in two different countries in order to be eligible for retirement benefits in one or both countries. The retirement benefits paid by each country are prorated based on the number of years worked there.

Totalization agreements are not alien to the United States. They currently have such agreements with Australia, Austria, Belgium, Canada, Chile, the Czech Republic, Denmark, Finland, France, Germany, Greece, Hungary, Ireland, Italy, Japan, Luxembourg, Netherlands, Norway, Poland, Portugal, the Slovak Republic, South Korea, Spain, Sweden, Switzerland, and the United Kingdom.

Steven Weiser, a tax lawyer with a practice focusing on international tax matters, explained how these totalization agreements work:

> *"For example, if an individual accumulates six years of coverage under the U.S. social security system and ten years of coverage in another country's system that requires 15 years of coverage for full benefit eligibility, both countries will treat the*

individual as if a total of 16 years had been completed under each system. However, the U.S. benefit would be 5/16 of the benefit computed on the basis of earnings in both countries during the 15-year period (and 10/16 in the other country)."

Regardless of the final shape of any agreement on Social Security, it is important to mention that, if the United States fails to negotiate in good faith on this issue or if they fail to honor their obligations to hard-working Texans who have paid into their system, Texas will always take care of its most vulnerable citizens. The total amount of federal money that comes back to Texas annually for federal pension benefits is approximately $74 billion. This is far short of the $120-$160 billion annually that we overpay into the federal system that will now stay here in Texas. In short, if they choose the immoral route, we've got it covered.

MILITARY AND DEFENSE

The issues that will consume the majority of the negotiations between the United States and a post-Texit Texas are, without a doubt, the issues of the military and defense. This fact has not gone unnoticed by Texit skeptics who can't decide whether the military will be sent to kill everyone who voted for Texit or will close down all military bases in Texas, thereby wrecking the economies of the surrounding communities. While both fears are completely irrational, they subconsciously recognize how thorny this issue will be.

Texas is currently home to 15 military installations with an economic impact of around $150 billion. However, the military installations account for only $14 billion in federal payroll spending in Texas. In addition, there are currently more than 118,000 Texans on active duty status across all branches of the military. These are not insignificant figures.

However, it is important not to conflate the issues of military presence and political union. The United States maintains nearly 800 military bases in more than 70 countries and territories abroad. No one would argue that those 70 countries are in a political union with the United States due to the presence of a U.S. military base, nor would anyone argue that they should be. The presence of these military bases on foreign soil is solely about shared defense concerns and security interests.

After a Texit, Texas may not share a government with the rest of the United States, but we will still share defense and national security concerns. International military cooperation has been a cornerstone of U.S. defense policy since the Second World War and, while it has been suggested that there should be some reforms, the underlying policy is unlikely to change, especially close to home.

It is, therefore, highly probable that Texas would enter into a mutual defense pact with the United States that includes joint use and operation of existing military bases and facilities in Texas. As a part of any mutual defense pact, Texas will likely have to pledge to spend a set percentage of its GDP on national defense, much like the reforms proposed for NATO. In return, the United States should guarantee the availability of military arms and equipment for tariff-free purchase by manufacturers in the United States and vice versa. Texas should stipulate that the mutual defense pact should only extend to commonly agreed defense concerns.

Any mutual defense pact of this nature could set a transition period where things essentially stay as they are now, operating under a joint command, until such time as the already established Texas military forces are at full readiness.

While this is fine for moving forward, there is still the issue of the now-foreign Texans who are currently serving in the U.S. military. There is already federal policy in place that governs non-citizens in the military. Every year, more than 8,000 non-citizens enlist in the armed forces. In addition, because of existing international treaties, citizens of the Federated States of Micronesia, the Republic of the Marshall Islands and Palau are allowed to enlist and regularly do so, as are Canadian citizens of Native American heritage. It is reasonable to assume that the United States military would want to extend this existing policy to cover the 118,000 Texans who currently serve, and likely any other Texans who would want to in the future.

NATIONAL DEBT

When it comes to the national debt, there is no softening the blow. When Texas leaves, it will have to take its share of the national debt with it. If the negotiations regarding the military win the prize for taking the most, the negotiations over the national debt will win the prize for being the most contentious. After all, in any divorce, outside of custody battles over children, money is the most heated issue. This will be no different.

In *Dismantling Confederation: The Divisive Question of the National Debt*, Paul Boothe looked at this issue in the event of Quebec exiting Canada. In it, he stated that division of public national debt "is considered one of the toughest and longest negotiation subjects during state secessions."

The contention will come in calculating Texas' share of the debt. It is highly unlikely that there will be any easy agreement on the issue. For example, the United States will likely demand that we take the national debt and divide that figure by the total population of the United States to get the per person share of the debt. In 2016, the gross federal debt amounted to around $60,470 per person. By multiplying that figure by the population of Texas, you arrive at an amount just shy of $1.7 trillion. I'm fairly certain they'll send us an invoice.

Texas will likely counter that we have paid substantially more into the federal system than we have gotten out of it for decades. Using the most conservative figure of $103 billion annually in overpayment, 16 years of overpayment should pretty much wipe the slate clean. Throw that on top of the fact that, while the federal government was busy exploding the national debt and spending like a drunken sailor on shore leave, Texas has been one of the prime drivers of economic growth for the entire United States. That doesn't even take into account that a large portion of the debt came from funding programs Texans didn't want or need or was wasted by federal mismanagement and inefficiency.

It is evident just from these viewpoints that any negotiation over the national debt and Texas' liability for its share will be exceptionally heated and, unless cooler heads prevail, could have detrimental effects on both Texas and the United States. The effects were highlighted in the 1997 essay by Daniel Blum entitled *The Apportionment of Public Debt and Assets during State Secession* published in the *Case Western Reserve Journal of International Law*. Blum noted that:

> *"Extended bargaining over the apportionment of the public debt and assets could prove costly because cool-headed calculations may not be easily made during heated secession negotiations. A heated debate between the seceding state and the parent state over the apportionment of the public debt and assets could affect both states' international credibility rating. Additional activities hurt by a prolonged debate include future trade between the two states and the states' participation in financial markets. A quick agreement between the seceding state and the parent state on the apportionment of debt and assets is imperative to a smooth, peaceful, and inexpensive transition to independence."*

Although there is no established international law that would compel Texas to pay anything, it will most likely want to. It has been customary throughout the world that, when a state secedes from a larger country or confederation, it voluntary accepts a portion of the national debt. This was the case with Singapore leaving Malaysia in 1965 and Bangladesh when it left Pakistan in 1971.

Blum's additional observations on the matter point to why Texas should follow suit.

"Economic and political realities usually compel the seceding state to voluntarily assume its share of the public debt. For instance, when Ukraine seceded from the former Soviet Union, Ukraine initially refused to pay any part of the Soviet Union's outstanding debt. However, for four months no other country would loan money to Ukraine until it finally agreed to pay its share of the Soviet debt. As a result, a seceding state may desire to voluntarily assume a portion of the public debt to portray itself as a respectable borrower in international financial markets."

Although the 1983 Vienna Convention on Succession of State in Respect of State Property, Archives and Debts attempted to establish an internationally recognized framework to deal with this issue, it only ended up establishing that a seceding state had an obligation to assume a portion of the debt in the absence of any superseding agreement between the two parties. It didn't, however, expound on how that portion should be calculated.

Blum's essay identified four different methods that can be used for calculation. The first is the per capita approach previously explored. The second is the GDP approach, which takes the State's percentage of the overall GDP with that percentage used as the percentage of national debt that's assumed. For Texas that would be somewhere between 9 percent and 10 percent on average, amounting to approximately $2 trillion. The third approach, which was explored earlier, is called the Historical Benefits Approach, where the amount of money paid into the federal system by the State is compared with the amount of money that has been paid by the federal system into the State. This ratio is applied as a percentage to the national debt and is the amount owed. In the case of Texas, our portion of the national debt would be $0.

Blum refers to the final method as the Historical Tax Shares Approach, which he explains in his essay.

> *"The rationale for the historical tax shares approach is that the seceding state must assume full responsibility for obligations of the federal government to its own citizens, and the seceding state's debt cannot be calculated independently of the asset side of the balance sheet. Hence, this method utilizes a balance-sheet approach by matching federal assets with liabilities. All federal assets are evaluated and each asset is allocated to a portion of the debt incurred. As a result, a link is formed between the assets and debt, requiring the payment of the debt to be the same percentage as the amount of the assets received. The seceding state should assume a dollar of debt for every dollar of assets that the seceding state takes. If the amount of assets apportioned to the seceding state is greater or less than the amount of debt apportioned to the seceding state, the amount of debt actually assumed by the seceding state is raised or lowered to equalize the seceding state's share of the public debt and assets."*

This method is the most difficult to calculate for both parties and impossible to calculate with any certainty, given the lack of financial accountability on the part of the federal government.

The simple fact is that there is no easy way to predict how negotiations over the national debt will play out or if there can ever be consensus over the issue. What is known is that until there is a Texit, Texas' share of the national debt will continue to climb. For Texas to be successful on the other side of this issue, it must negotiate in good faith and must signal its willingness to pay its fair share of the national debt, even if that share is $0.

238

THE REST

It cannot be overemphasized that independence is a state of being to which an independent Texas will continue to aspire. It is not a rejection of interconnectedness. Rather, it is an acknowledgement that Texans can work with other self-governing nations as peers.

There will certainly be other issues that arise during the transition from State to nation-state. But, as we've seen with what are usually considered the "major" issues, there are already laws, policies, and international norms that exist to cover every eventuality and Texas is well-suited for the challenge. While Texit may raise issues that seem insurmountable to some, they have been experienced and solved by people all over the world. And it is always important to remember the Texas proverb: "If you want something done, tell a Texan that it can't be done."

8 | THE FUTURE REPUBLIC OF TEXAS

> **"**Self government is our right, a thing born in us at birth, a thing no more to be doled out to us, or withheld from us, by another people than the right to life itself...**"**
>
> *Roger Casement*

There is only one concrete issue in the Texit debate. We know with near certainty what will happen if Texas stays in the Union. The middle class will continue to shrink. The national debt will exceed the entire ability of the American people to produce, driving the federal government into bankruptcy. Federal programs will collapse as the government loses the ability to pay for them. Inflation will skyrocket as the government cranks up the printing presses to create more money out of thin air. The cultural divide will widen and an increase of civil unrest is almost assured. Trade imbalances will drive manufacturers overseas. Federal regulations will continue to grow at a rapid pace, forcing small businesses to shutter their doors and discouraging the creation of new businesses to replace them, thus eliminating the opportunity to move up the socioeconomic ladder.

What we cannot do, however, is predict with 100 percent certainty what an independent Texas will look like, nor should we follow

Scotland's example and put forth a political manifesto as though it were destiny. There is one main reason why absolute certainty in this matter is problematic.

This generation of Texans has never operated outside the context of the federal system. Therefore, until independence becomes a reality for the people of Texas or, at a minimum, is evident, everything will be viewed through the lens of our skewed federal perspective. Operating outside the federal system opens up opportunities to address challenges and approach governance in ways that Texans never imagined. The great promise of Texit is that it puts all options on the table, especially those we never had before. One doesn't need to know the source of the light to know that it's bright. So it goes with predicting the future of an independent Republic of Texas.

Often overlooked is the increased level of political engagement by the people that comes ahead of and behind votes for self-determination. Voter turnout rates in Texas are traditionally low. In the 2016 general election, Texas experienced an abnormally high turnout of 59.39 percent. However, two years previous, in a non-presidential election year, turnout was 33.70 percent. Historically, independence referenda drive greater than an 85 percent voter turnout. For the time leading up to the vote, people become politically engaged and well informed on matters of public policy and governance.

On the other side of a successful vote for Texit, you have an energized, knowledgeable people that are no longer distracted by the dog-and-pony show of federal politics. More voices and more ideas will be injected into the conversation on how to best govern an independent Texas. And now the "big show" will move from Washington to Austin, where the eyes of Texas will truly be upon those elected to serve the public trust. No longer able to hide in obscurity, their actions will be closely scrutinized. This greater scrutiny will bring greater accountability. With the inability to draw campaign funds from special interests outside of Texas, politicians will be forced to look toward home for support, to their constituents. Those constituents, for the first time in their lives, will have the power of self-government.

With the power of self-government and near limitless opportunity in our hands, we can try to predict what that possible future could look like, based on what we currently know about the issues Texans feel strongest about and the attitudes they have toward those issues. In this, Texans are not bashful and have given strong indicators as to the direction they would like to see taken in public policy.

There is an abundance of polling data about the attitudes of Texans on what have been considered federal issues that is particularly useful. The University of Texas, in conjunction with the *Texas Tribune,* regularly polls Texans on public policy issues. We can also look at legislation, both proposed and passed, as well as the platforms of candidates that were supported by Texans and in what proportions they were supported.

There are some issues common to all independent nations that are all handled in virtually the same way. A good example of this is the issue of the military and national defense. All independent nations have a military. While the size, composition, and budget may differ, they are all essentially variations on a theme. International travel, banking, and air traffic control are other examples.

In addition, there are issues where there are precedents that give a strong indication as to what will happen. For example, an unusually common question is whether Texas professional sports teams will still play in their respective leagues. Major League Baseball already allows non-U.S. teams with the Toronto Blue Jays, the National Hockey League does it with teams in both Canada and the United States, and the National Football League has recently discussed expanding into

Mexico and the U.K. Ultimately, that will be their decision. However, if you follow the money, it becomes a safe bet that Texas teams will still be playing in their respective leagues post-Texit.

To quote the conservative firebrand and Texit advocate, Claver Kamau-Imani, "After Texit, we're gonna be rich!" He's not exaggerating. Texas already collectively possesses a fair amount of wealth as one of the largest economies in the world. However, Texit promises to bring that wealth to every citizen of Texas. In exploring the negative effect of excessive federal regulations on Texans, the cited study showed how it has shrunk the paychecks of Texans by 75 percent. Flip the script and look at it from the standpoint of a Texas no longer subjected to those excessive federal regulations. Over time, the average Texan could see a 400 percent increase in take-home pay.

The retention of this type of wealth by Texans translates into an explosion of new business startups and corporate expansions, reducing unemployment to near zero. Texas can experience double-digit economic growth as the lack of an income tax turns Texas into an international haven for wealth and foreign investment. All of this economic activity results in an increase in government revenue, leading to better schools, improved infrastructure, and additional tax breaks.

The best data available shows a correlation between increased consumer spending and an increase of household income at a near 1:1 ratio. With these kinds of numbers, Texas could eliminate the property tax, leave the sales tax rate untouched and still produce an increase in government revenue over and above what Texans currently pay to both the state and federal governments.

Texans are not opposed to sensible immigration. In fact, Texas celebrates the diversity that immigration brings. What Texans do want, however, is for those who emigrate to do so properly and in a manner consistent with the needs of Texas. On the issue of immigration, Texas has always sought a sustainable equilibrium. It is reasonable to assume that Texas would implement a sensible immigration policy that allows immigration based on the ability of Texas to handle the increased infrastructure requirements and the need to supplement the pool of skilled workers required for business and industry. Citizens would be given priority in employment, with immigration used to supplement shortages in key job sectors. Concretely addressing the immigration and security concerns of Texans leads to greater confidence in our institutions, frees up public sector expenditure, and leads to better relations with our neighbor to the south.

Texas has always shown a belief in a strong national defense, with a focus on threats to the safety and security of Texans at home. An independent Texas has little in the way of conventional national security concerns. The threat of a combined land, air, and sea invasion is next to non-existent. But threats do still exist. There is the threat of the cartels and violence spilling over our border with Mexico as well as the threat of international terrorists using that same border to execute attacks on civilian targets within Texas. In addition, there are always threats that could upset international stability. While these are often met with the combined military might of the western world, an independent Texas would be ready and willing to do its part.

The bulk of Texas national defense will be concentrated on three key areas: strengthening the borders against national security risks, defense against attack from international state actors, and supporting military actions of allies that are congruent with our strategic objectives.

Using the NATO target average of 2 percent of GDP for military and defense spending would provide approximately $32.78 billion annually, making Texas 11th in the world in defense spending. Funding at this level would cover the costs of recruiting, training, equipping, and maintaining an active duty enlistment in excess of 125,000 troops.

This would be in line with the number of Texans currently serving in the United States military in all branches. In addition, it would provide a level of funding to, over time, increase our inventory of military vehicles including naval vessels, fighters and support aircraft, and armored vehicles. Building on the current military infrastructure in the Texas Military Department (TMD), Texas will grow the components of the TMD into a world-class military force capable of addressing any threat to the safety and security of Texas posed by any who would do us harm.

This is all just speculation, but it is a vision of Texas that is worth having. Imagine traveling anywhere in the world using your Texas passport and seeing the Texas flag flying above our embassies and consulates. Or imagine cheering on Team Texas in the Olympics as they stand alongside competitors from nations around the world.

This is what it's like to be a self-governing nation among other self-governing nations, and it is what's waiting on the other side of Texit.

9 | OVERCOMING THE REAL CHALLENGES FACING TEXIT

66 There would be no difficulty in securing the rights of the people and the liberties of Texas if men would march to their duty and not fly like recreants from danger. Texas must be defended and liberty maintained. 99

Sam Houston

When the modern-day Texit movement really began in 1996, those who signed on, in excess of several hundred thousand, renounced their citizenship in the United States and swore an oath of allegiance to the Republic of Texas. Every one of them did so willingly. They were ready, in that moment, to give up something that no longer aligned with their ideals and begin the hard work of building a new nation.

They were full of questions. To paraphrase cosmologist Max Tegmark, they would rather have questions they couldn't answer than answers they couldn't question. More important, they were full of the hope that having a clean slate can bring. Not every question had an answer, but they knew they would finally have the power to determine what those answers would be. They wanted something better than the status quo. Without hesitation or reservation they, each for their own reasons, embraced a future that none of them could actually touch or see but one they could feel. They were motivated by something they had never experienced in their lives—a real chance to create their own destiny.

To understand why and how Texas will eventually leave the Union, this is the only thing one needs to know. Hope for a better future has driven more people to exercise their right of self-determination than any other factor. This is why Texit is not an easily understood social or political phenomenon. At the risk of sounding esoteric, it is something spiritual. Texans understand it but have difficulty articulating it. It lives somewhere "out there" but it also lives deep in the heart of Texans. It has political and economic motivations and aspirations, yet also exists within the long-woven cultural threads that bind all Texans together. It is forward thinking and looks to the horizon, yet never forgets that its spirit is the legacy of the victorious dead at Goliad, the Alamo, and San Jacinto.

While some have accused Texit supporters of running from the fight of "saving America," Texans view it as preserving what was great about American principles and spirit as it faces extinction in the land it once called home. Shunned by those who were once countrymen to preserve those principles, Texas will leave the Union.

Texit is an acknowledgement of the fundamental problem in 21st century America—one size does not fit all. What is best for Texas and Texans is not necessarily what is best for every State in the Union. It is this one-size-fits-all mentality that derailed the American Union in the first place. It is the creed of unabashed allegiance to a system that uses the federal government as a weapon to impose the political will of a select group upon everyone else. Federal elections have degenerated into contests for who gets to wield the club and bash the loser into submission. Texit says there's a better way than the status quo. Let California be California. Let New York be New York. Let Texas be Texas.

Texit is not adversarial, though. It acknowledges our shared history with the other States. It says let's be friends and engage in commerce and travel. It says that, if a true external threat exists for one, it exists for all of us, and channeling the spirit of the Texian Army, we have your back. However, when it comes to how we govern ourselves, we've got that covered.

Within this vision of the future resides one great lie that underpins the sense of urgency expressed by those who support Texit. Where the federal government is concerned, the status quo is a myth. There is no rolling back the clock and returning the United States to the vision of its Founders. There is no way to put the genie back into the bottle. The federal government is on a course that will see every grievance multiplied and every ill intensified over time until every pretense of being a federative republic is finally abandoned and any illusion of a hopeful return to the way it was "supposed to be" is shattered. It is the natural order of things. Therefore, Texans should take the words of G.K. Chesterton to heart when he said, "People talk about the impatience of the populace; but sound historians know that most tyrannies have been possible because men moved too late."

Texit advocates are moving forward. The growth of the Texit movement parallels many political and social movements throughout the ages. First ridiculed and scorned, then feared and shunned, Texit is now a part of mainstream political dialogue. It rests firmly in the pantheon of modern-day independence movements and can stand shoulder to shoulder with them as all struggle for the fundamental right of self-government.

Many years ago, while still trying to fully comprehend and put into words what has become known as Texit, I came across a passage from Irish politician and author Terence McSwiney. Although written about the Irish and their drive for independence, I believe the spirit of it applies to Texans and their desire for independence. It explains that independence really isn't about the technical minutiae, monetary and trade policy or any number of issues that often hog the debate. Rather, it comes from a place much deeper and much harder to quantify, and it is from that place that the destiny of Texas will be written.

> *"Let us grow big with our cause. Shall we honour the flag we bear by a mean, apologetic front? No! Wherever it is down, lift it; wherever it is challenged, wave it; wherever it is high, salute it; wherever it is victorious, glorify and exult in it. At all times and forever be for it proud, passionate, persistent, jubilant, defiant; stirring hidden memories, kindling old fires, wakening the finer instincts of men, till all are one in the old spirit, the spirit that will not admit defeat, that has been voiced by thousands, that is noblest in Emmet's one line, setting the time for his epitaph: "When my country"—not if—but "when my country takes her place among the nations of the earth." It is no hypothesis; it is a certainty. There have been in every generation, and are in our own, men dull of apprehension and cold of heart, who could not believe this, but we believe it, we live in it: we know it. Yes, we know it, as Emmet knew it, and as it shall be seen to-morrow; and when the historian of to-morrow, seeing it accomplished, will write its history, he will not note the end with surprise."*

GLOSSARY OF TERMS

Articles of Confederation: The agreement among 13 original states of United States of America that served as its first Constitution.

Bank charter: A charter authorizing the operation of a bank.

Bilateral agreement: A bilateral agreement involves two parties, each promising to do something. The parties can be individuals, groups, businesses or governments. Somehow, the two actions are mutually supportive, binding and inclusive. Both parties fulfill roles as the promisor and the promisee. A bilateral agreement can be "positive" or "negative"—you "will" or "will not" do something. Each party is sufficient consideration for the bilateral agreement. The concept of "mutuality" is important for bilateral agreements since both parties must fulfill their promise for the contract to be fulfilled.

Bill of Attainder: An act of the legislature that declares a person, or group of persons, guilty of crime and punishes them, often without a trial.

Bloc: A combination of countries, parties or groups that share a common purpose.

Chartered bank: A chartered bank is a financial institution, whose primary role is to accept and safeguard monetary deposits from individuals and organizations, and to lend money out. Chartered bank specifics vary from country to country; however, in general, a chartered bank in operation has obtained a form of government permission to do business in the financial services industry.

Chuse: Choose (archaic).

Conflate: To fuse into one entity, i.e., to conflate dissenting voices into one protest.

Contemporaneous: Existing or occurring in the same period of time.

Contiguous: Sharing a common border; touching.

Currency Union: A currency union (also known as a monetary union) involves two or more states sharing the same currency without them necessarily having any further integration (such as an economic and monetary union, which would have, in addition, a customs union and a single market); see also **Informal currency union, Formal currency union**, and **Formal currency union currency with common policy** in this glossary.

Customs union: A type of trade bloc composed of free trade areas with common external tariffs; common external trade policy between countries, but different import quotas.

Despotism: A form of government in which a single entity rules with absolute power. Normally, that entity is an individual, the despot, as in an autocracy, but societies that limit respect and power to specific groups have also been called despotic.

Economic union: A type of trade bloc composed of a common market with a customs union; both participating countries have common policies on product regulation, freedom of movement of goods, services and the factors of production and a common external trade policy.

Eschew: Deliberately avoid using; abstain from.

Ex post facto Law: A law that makes an act illegal that was legal when it was committed, or which increases the infraction after it has been committed, or which changes the rules of evidence to make the conviction easier; prohibited by the U.S. Constitution.

Expound: To present and explain systematically, and in detail.

Fiscal policy: Fiscal policy is the means by which a government adjusts its spending levels and tax rates to monitor and influence a nation's economy. It is the sister strategy to monetary policy through which a central bank influences a nation's money supply. These two policies are used in various combinations to direct a country's economic goals.

Formal currency union: A currency union with common policy, established by multiple countries of a common monetary policy, that issues authority for their common currencies.

Free trade agreement: Cooperation between at least two countries to reduce trade barriers, import quotas and tariffs, and increase trade of goods and services with each other.

Geopolitical trends: Trends that study the influence of geography, economics and demography on politics, and the influence of foreign policy on a state.

Impinge: To have an effect or impact on (especially negative).

Informal currency union: A currency union with a unilateral adoption of foreign currency by one of the participating nations.

Interstate bank branching: Accepting deposits or making loans away from the home office bank and across state lines.

Member states: A state that is a member of an international organization or a federation or confederation; they must agree unanimously to adopt policies.

Monetary policy: Actions of a central bank, currency board or other regulatory committee that determine the size and rate of growth of the money supply, which then affects interest rates.

Monolithic: Large, powerful and intractably indivisible and uniform.

Multilateral agreement: An exchange agreement between three or more parties, agencies or governments; has a bigger impact than bilateral agreements.

NAFTA (North American Free Trade Agreement): An agreement signed by Canada, Mexico, the United States, creating a trilateral bloc in North America.

Nation-state: A country where a distinct cultural or ethnic group inhabit a territory and have formed a state that they predominantly govern.

Negotiated currency union: (formal with common policy) A currency union established by multiple countries with common monetary policy and issuing authority for their common currency.

Negotiated trade agreement: A wide-ranging tax, tariff and trade treaty that often includes investment guarantees brought into effect by negotiation.

Official currency unions: Today, there are more than twenty official currency unions: The most used is the euro, which is used by 19 of the 28 members of the European Union; the U.S. dollar, which is the official currency in the U.S., Puerto Rico, El Salvador and many others; and the Swiss franc, which is official in Switzerland and Lichtenstein.

Political activism: Political activism includes individual and collective actions in support of a political position, including activities commonly associated with political campaigns.

Political union: A type of state composed of or created of, smaller states or political entities joined as one.

Prognosticator: Someone who forecasts or predicts the future from present indications or signs.

Progressivism: The support for, or advocacy of, improvement of society by reform.

Ratification clause: In this book, referring to Article VII of the United States Constitution, which states: "The Ratification of the Conventions of nine States, shall be sufficient for the Establishment of this Constitution between the States so ratifying the Same."

Referendum: A general vote by the electorate on a single political question referred to them for a direct decision.

Secessionist: A person who favors formal withdrawal from membership of a federation or body, especially a political state.

Self-determination: The process by which a country determines its own statehood and forms its own allegiances and government.

Singular external trade policy: Laws related to the exchange of one good or service traded with foreign countries.

Supranational: Beyond the authority of one national government (usually an alliance involving three or more countries for their mutual benefit).

Texas Nationalist Movement (TNM): The Texas Nationalist Movement, under the leadership of President Daniel Miller, works to promote, secure and protect the political, cultural and economic independence of the nation of Texas, to restore and protect a constitutional Republic of Texas, to defend the inherent and inalienable rights of the people of Texas and promote the values of Texas nationalism. TNM claims to work peacefully with the current political system and rejects the use of force to achieve its goals. TNM focuses on political support, advocacy and education surrounding the issue of secession.

Texit: Based on the word "exit", a worldwide movement focusing, in this instance, on the possibility of a Texas exit from the U.S.

White papers: A government or other authoritative report giving information or proposals on an issue.

World Trade Organization tariff schedules: Schedules of custom duties on merchandise imports, created by the World Trade Organization (WTO), which deals with global rules of trade between nations.

BIBLIOGRAPHY

AIR Worldwide. "AIR Worldwide Estimates $65B – $75B in Texas Property Damage from Harvey Flooding." 6 September 2017. *AIR Worldwide web site.*

ALBERTSON, JOSHUA BLANK AND BETHANY. "Polling Center: Texan First, American Second." 3 April 2014. *texastribune.com.*

Anderson, Tom. "Study: 41 percent expect no Social Security benefits." 22 May 2015. *CNBC.com.*

Applebome, Peter. "Bench Mark: Divided We Stand; If at First You Don't Secede . . ." *New York Times* 26 November 2000.

Asthana, Anushka and Rowena Mason. "Barack Obama: Brexit would put UK 'back of the queue' for trade talks." 22 April 2016. *The Guardian.*

Baddour, Dylan. "Texas GOP official wants secession on the primary ballot." *Houston Chronicle* 25 November 2015.

Baer, Josette. "Who, Why and How : Assessing the Legitimacy of Secession." *Swiss Political Science Review* (2000): 48.

Bailey, Ronald. "Federal Regulations Have Made You 75 Percent Poorer." 21 June 2013. *Reason.com.*

Baldwin, Ian and Frank Bryan. "The Once and Future Republic of Vermont." 1 April 2007. *Washington Post.*

Batkins, Sam. "How Many Federal Forms Are There?" 21 April 2016. *American Action Forum web site.*

Beckel, Michael. "Americans For Prosperity Spent Record Cash In 2012." 14 November 2013. *Huffington Post.*

Bellamy, Francis. "National School Celebration of Columbus Day: The Official Programme." *The Youth's Companion* 8 September 1892.

Bender, Bryan. "Pentagon credit cards used for gambling, escorts." 6 May 2015. *Politico.com.*

Benson, Guy. "To Infinity and Beyond: New Polls Show Americans Want Magical Government Benefits, Oppose All Spending Cuts." 25 April 2017. *Townhall.*

Black, Andrew. "Scottish independence: Referendum White Paper unveiled." 26 November 2013. *BBC News.*

Black, Henry Campbell. *A Dictionary of Law: Containing Definitions of the Terms and Phrases of American and English Jurisprudence, Ancient and Modern.* 1891.

Bloomberg Businessweek. "One Nation Divisible." 15 September 2016.

Blum, Daniel S. "The Apportionment of Public Debt and Assets during State Secession." *Case Western Reserve Journal of International Law* (1997).

Blum, Daniel. "The Apportionment of Public Debt and Assets during State Secession." *Case Western Reserve Journal of International Law* (1997).

Boothe, Paul, Barbara Johnston and Karrin Powys-Lybbe. "Dismantling Confederation: The Divisive Question of the National Debt." *Closing The Books, Canada Round Series no. 8.* C.D. Howe Institute, 1991. 26-55.

Burt, Andrew. "'These United States': How Obama's Vocal Tic Reveals a Polarized America." 13 May 2013. *The Atlantic.*

Carr, Snapper. "The Texas Legislative Process: The "Real" Story!" *2010 TCAA Summer Conference Speaker Papers.* Texas City Attorneys Association, 2010.

Center For Responsive Politics. "Donor Demographics." n.d. *OpenSecrets.org.* 20 January 2018.

Chibber, Kabir. "Here are all the countries that don't have a currency of their own." 15 September 2014. *Quartz.*

Clausewitz, Carl von. *On War.* 1832.

Clyde Wayne Crews, Jr. *Ten Thousand Commandments.* Competitive Enterprise Institute, 2017.

Cohn, Scott. "New study names America's most regulated states." 29 March 2016. *CNBC.com.*

Congressional Budget Office. "Federal Grants to State and Local Governments." 2013. cbo.gov.

Corps, United States Marine. *Warfighting.* Cosimo Reports, 2007.

Crews, Clyde Wayne. "Nobody Knows How Many Federal Agencies Exist." 26 August 2015. *Competitive Enterprise Institute.*

DANN, CARRIE. "Poll: A Record Number of Americans Say Government 'Should Do More'." 23 April 2017. *NBC News.*

DeMarco, Gabrielle. "Minority Rules: Scientists Discover Tipping Point for the Spread of Ideas." 25 July 2011. *Rensselaer Polytechnic Institute (RPI).*

Department of Homeland Security. "U.S. Visa Waiver Program." n.d. *dhs.gov.* 20 January 2018.

Dyer, C.E. "BREAKING: Texas Gov. Makes Announcement About Secession." 27 June 2016. *Conservative Tribune.*

Edwards, Chris. "Federal Government Pay Exceeds Most Industries." 5 October 2015. *Cato Institute web site.*

Eggen, Dan. "Federal Credit Cards Misused." 9 April 2008. *WashingtonPost.com.*

Ehley, Brianna. "Lawmakers Lash Out at Agencies for Paying $3.1 Billion to Idle Workers." 22 October 2014. *The Fiscal Times.*

Elliot, Jonathan. "DEBATES IN THE CONVENTION OF THE COMMONWEALTH OF MASSACHUSETTS, ON THE ADOPTION OF THE FEDERAL CONSTITUTION." *The Debates in the Several State Conventions on the Adoption of the Federal Constitution* (1836): vol.2, page 46.

Essig, Chris, Aditi Bhandari and Jolie McCullough. "Here's how much Texas candidates spent per vote in the November elections." 1 March 2017. *The Texas Tribune.*

Farage, Nigel. "FARAGE – Let's Get Real: Would Obama Unconditionally Open Borders To Mexico As We've Done With The EU? No Chance!" 22 April 2016. *Breitbart.*

Farley, Robert. "What Perry Really Said About Secession." 23 August 2011. *Factcheck.org.*

Fernandez, Manny. "White House Rejects Petitions to Secede, but Texans Fight On." *New York Times* 15 January 2013.

Fields, Gary and John R. Emshwiller. "Many Failed Efforts to Count Nation's Federal Criminal Laws." 23 July 2011. *Wall Street Journal.*

Finkelman, Paul. "How the Civil War Changed the Constitution." 2 June 2015. *New York Times.*

Fletcher, Nick. "FTSE 100 now above pre-Brexit vote levels." 29 June 2016. *The Guardian.*

FORAN, CLARE. "How Can the U.S. Fix a Broken Government?" 16 July 2016. *The Atlantic.*

Fox News. "NIH Funds $2.6 Million Study to Get Prostitutes in China to Drink Less." 14 May 2009. *Foxnews.com.*

"No 'Texit': Trump says Texas 'will never' secede, amid renewed calls." 25 June 2016. *foxnews.com.*

FoxBusiness. "US national debt tops $20T for first time in history." 11 September 2017. *Fox Business web site.*

Gaines, Jim. "One in four Americans want their state to secede from the U.S., but why?" 19 September 2014. *reuters.com.* 20 September 2014.

Gass, Nick. "Trump reports $35.8 million raised in July." 1 August 2016. *Politico.*

"GENERAL APPROPRIATIONS ACT for the 2018-19 BIENNIUM: Text of Conference Committee Report on Senate Bill No. 1." n.d. *Texas Legislative Budget Board.* 23 October 2017.

Gold, Matea. "Clinton campaign had best fundraising month yet, with $63 million haul in July." 2 August 2016. *The Washington Post.*

Goodwin, Matthew. "Ukip's days of amateur campaigning are over." 17 November 2014. *The Telegraph.*

Gordon, Tom. "One year on: will Better Together change their tactics?" 22 June 2013. *The Herald.*

Governing. "Military Active-Duty Personnel, Civilians by State." n.d. *Governing.com.* 20 January 2018.

Hamilton, Alexander. "The Same Subject Continued: Concerning the General Power of Taxation." *Daily Advertiser* 3 January 1788.

Harris, Aaron. "Hill County – What Happened?" 5 January 2018. *Direct Action Texas.*

Hill, Kashmir. "TSA Threatens To Cancel All Flights Out Of Texas If 'Groping Bill' Passed." 25 May 2011. *Forbes.com.*

"How many members does NOW currently have?" n.d. *National Organization for Women.*

Howard, Philip K. "Reform Is Not Enough: The Federal Government Needs a Complete Makeover." 3 August 2012. *theatlantic.com.*

Huntington, Samuel P. *The Clash of Civilizations and the Remaking of World Order.* Simon & Schuster, 2011.

Ingraham, Christopher. "Most gun owners don't belong to the NRA and they don't agree with it either." 15 October 2015. *The Washington Post.*

"Internal Revenue Service Data Book, 2015." n.d. *IRS.gov.* Statistics of Income Division, Communications and Data Dissemination Section.

Internal Revenue Service. "Totalization Agreements." n.d. *IRS.gov.* 20 January 2018.

International Monetary Fund. "Report for Selected Country Groups and Subjects." 2015.

Jakab, András, Arthur Dyevre and Giulio Itzcovich. *Comparative Constitutional Reasoning.* Cambridge University Press, 2017.

Jones, Jeffrey M. "Government Dissatisfaction Returns as Most Important Problem." 9 February 2017. *Gallup News.*

Jonsson, Patrik. "Why is Texas always a mere Fort Sumter away from seceding?" 24 November 2012. *Christian Science Monitor.*

Kibbe, Matt and Timothy Head. "Too Many Laws Means Too Many Criminals." 21 May 2015. *National Review.*

Larson, Carlton F.W. "Five myths about treason." *The Washington Post* 17 February 2017.

Layton, Peter. "The 2 Percent NATO Benchmark Is a Red Herring." 16 February 2017. *The National Interest.*

League of United Latin American Citizens. "About Us." n.d. *lulac. org.* 20 01 2018.

Light, Paul C. *Thickening Government: Federal Hierarchy and the Diffusion of Accountability.* Brookings, 1995.

Lucas, Fred. "IRS Rehires 213 Employees Ousted for Falsifying Documents, Avoiding Taxes, Other Offenses." 14 August 2017. *dailysignal.com.*

Madison, James. "The Conformity of the Plan to Republican Principles." *Independent Journal* 18 January 1788.

"The Same Subject Continued: The Powers Conferred by the Constitution Further Considered." *Independent Journal* 23 January 1788.

Martin, Phillip. "Research 2000 Poll: Half of Texas Republicans Want to Secede." 23 April 2009. *burntorangereport.com.*

McClanahan, Dr. Brion. "Secession: The American Tradition." 24 January 2015. *Mises Institute.*

McLaughlin, Patrick. "Regulations Contribute to Poverty: Testimony before the House Committee on the Judiciary, Subcommittee on Regulatory Reform, Commercial and Antitrust Law." 24 February 2016. *Mercatus Center George Mason University.*

McLawsen, Greg. "Can immigrants serve in the US military? 8 Q&As about non-citizen service." 6 September 2017. *AvvoStories.*

McPherson, Kevin and Bruce Wright. "Federal Funding in Texas." November 2017. *Texas Office of the Comptroller.*

Miller, Daniel. "It's time for a showdown: convention of states vs. Texas independence." 19 September 2016. *TribTalk.*

MoneyTips. "Federal Employees Earn 50% More Than The Private Workforce." 21 12 2015. *HuffingtonPost.*

Murray, Iain. "Leviathan." 3 February 2011. *National Review web site.*

Murray, Teresa Dixon. "Sale of Citizens Bank leaves 44 foreign-owned banks that are FDIC-insured." 13 November 2015. *Cleveland Plain Dealer.*

"NAACP Passes Resolution Supporting Strong Clean Air Act." 4 August 2011. *naacp.org.*

Naisbitt, John. *Global Paradox.* Avon, 1995.

NARAL. *About Us.* n.d. 20 January 2018.

Nathan, Andrew J. "China at the Tipping Point? Foreseeing the Unforeseeable." *Journal of Democracy* (2013): 20-25.

National Conference of State Legislatures. "MILITARY'S IMPACT ON STATE ECONOMIES." 21 February 2017. *NCSL.org.*

O'Brien, Matt and Spencer Raley. "The Fiscal Burden of Illegal Immigration on United States Taxpayers." 2017.

Office of the Texas Governor. "Active Duty Military Installations." n.d. *Office of the Texas Governor.* 20 January 2018.

Office of the United States Trade Representative. "Free Trade Agreements." n.d. *Office of the United States Trade Representative.* 20 01 2018.

Patton, Mike. "National Debt Tops $18 Trillion: Guess How Much You Owe?" 24 April 2015. *Forbes.com.*

Pew Charitible Trusts. "Federal Spending in the States." 2016.

Powers, Rod. "Immigrants in the US Armed Forces." 8 September 2016. *The Balance.*

RAPPEPORT, ALAN. "I.R.S. Commissioner, Demonized by Conservatives, Leaves on His Terms." 5 November 2017. *New York Times.*

Reed, Brian. "SHOCKING: Six Projects You Won't Believe The Government Is Funding." 29 September 2011. *BusinessInsider. com.*

Riedl, Brian M. "How Your Government Wastes Your Money." 20 May 2005. *Heritage Foundation web site.*

Ritter, Karl. "Catalonia's divided residents head to the polls again." 20 December 2017. *Fox News.*

Robinson, Paul H. "Fair Notice and Fair Adjudication: Two Kinds of Legality." *Faculty Scholarship* (2005): Paper 601.

Rogers, Abby. "Sorry Secessionists, Justice Scalia Won't Help You Out." 15 November 2012. *Business Insider.*

Ross, Michael A. *Justice of Shattered Dreams: Samuel Freeman Miller and the Supreme Court during the Civil War Era.* LSU Press, 2003.

Saiidi, Uptin. "The Brexit ballot wording wasn't always so simple." 22 June 2016. *CNBC.*

Samuelson, Robert J. "FEDERAL DEBT: WHAT IF GOVERNMENTS CAN'T REPAY?" 28 October 2009. *Newsweek.*

Shannon, Kelley. "Democrats: Texas gov should disavow secession talk." 17 April 2009. *Associated Press.*

Sharp, Gene. *Sharp's Dictionary of Power and Struggle: Language of Civil Resistance in Conflicts.* Oxford University Press, 2011.

Siegner, Clint. "The Federal Government Won't Get Fixed Until It Breaks." 27 March 2017. *moneymetals.com.*

Swarts, Phillip. "Go home Uncle Sam, you're drunk! Feds rang up $1.3M booze tab last year." 20 March 2014. *Washington Times.*

Terkel, Amanda and Ryan Grim. "MoveOn Moving On: Progressive Powerhouse Launches Radical Strategic Overhaul." 4 December 2012. *Huffington Post.*

Texans for Lawsuit Reform. "ABOUT TLR." n.d. *tortreform.com.* 20 01 2018.

Texas Department of Public Safety. "Texas Criminal Alien Arrest Data." n.d. *Texas Department of Public Safety.* 11 08 2017.

Texas Legislative Council. n.d. web site. 20 January 2018.

Texas Nationalist Movement. "State Rep Gives Startling Response To #Texit Question." 31 August 2016. *Texas Nationalist Movement Web site.*

"Texas State Rep Candidate Comes Out In Support of Independence." 09 12 2015. *Texas Nationalist Movement Web site.*

Texas Politics Project at the University of Texas at Austin. n.d. September 2017.

Traynor, Ian. "Bush insists Kosovo must be independent and receives hero's welcome in Albania." 10 June 2007. *The Guardian.*

U.S. Chamber of Commerce. "About the U.S. Chamber of Commerce." n.d. *uschamber.com.* 20 January 2018.

United States Census Bureau. "State Exports from Texas." n.d. *United States Census Bureau.* 20 January 2018.

Valverde, Miriam. "Trump says 1 million legal crossings along U.S.-Mexico border." 14 September 2016. *Politifact.*

Vandevelder, Paul. "One nation—but maybe not so indivisible." 18 November 2012. *Los Angeles Times.*

Vine, David. "Where in the World Is the U.S. Military?" July 2015. *Politico.*

Weiser, Steven. "Understanding Social Security Tax, Totalization Agreements and Your Benefits." 21 May 2013. *Siskind Susser PC.*

Weller, Chris. "Hillary Clinton nearly ran for president on a policy of giving people unconditional free money." 12 September 2017. *Business Insider.*

Wilding, Peter. "Britain, a referendum and an ever-closer reckoning." 15 May 2012. *BlogActiv.eu.*

Zimmermann, Eric. "VIDEO: Paul says secession 'very American'." 20 April 2009. *thehill.com.*

Zogby, John. "Civil War Lives on in Our Politics." 20 April 2011. *Forbes.*

"The United States Of Discontent." 17 September 2009. *Forbes.*

About the Author

 Daniel Miller is president of the Texas Nationalist Movement and has been an outspoken advocate for Texas independence since 1996. As the head of one of the largest and most influential political organizations in Texas, Miller has extensively researched and engaged the issue of self-determination, not just for Texas, but as part of a growing global trend.

He has been featured on every major news network and been interviewed by every major newspaper in Texas and around the world. A featured guest on Fox News, CNN, CNBC, BBC News, RT-TV and many other news outlets, Miller has been a vocal proponent of a fundamental reexamination of the relationship between all states in the Union.

In 2011 he authored *Line in the Sand*, his first book, which addresses the roots of Texas nationalism and the practical implications of national self-identity for Texans. Taken from years of experience, *Line In The Sand*, has become a primer in the fundamentals of Texas nationalism.

Miller, a sixth generation Texan, was born and raised in Northeast Texas and currently resides in Southeast Texas with his wife, Cara. Both avid Texas Music fans, Daniel and Cara operate Radio Free Texas, one of the first online outlets for independent music created in Texas.

Made in the USA
Las Vegas, NV
16 December 2021

38265501R00163